The
California
Cookbook

Favorite Hometown Recipes from The Golden State

Cookbook Resources LLC
Highland Village, Texas

The California Cookbook
Favorite Hometown Recipes from The Golden State

1ˢᵗ Printing - June 2009

International Standard Book No. 978-1-59769-020-1

Library of Congress No. 2008022719

Library of Congress Cataloging-in-Publication Data

    The California cookbook : favorite hometown recipes from the Golden State / cover by Nancy Murphy Griffith ; illustrations by Nancy Bohanan.
     Includes index.
     ISBN-13: 978-1-59769-020-1
     ISBN-10: 1-59769-020-1
     1. Cookery, American--California style. I. Cookbook Resources, LLC. II. Title.
     TX715.2.C34C344 2008
     641.59794--dc22

                                 2008022719

Cover by Nancy Murphy Griffith
Illustrations by Nancy Bohanan

Manufactured in China and
Edited, Designed and Published in the United States of America by
Cookbook Resources, LLC
541 Doubletree Drive
Highland Village, Texas 75077

Toll free 866-229-2665

www.cookbookresources.com

Bringing Family and Friends to the Table

California Cuisine

California cuisine may be best summarized with the words fresh and diverse. With a climate that allows for growing fruits and vegetables all year long, it is easy to see how California's culinary traditions center around fresh foods. The staggering number of fruits and vegetables grown in the state almost makes "fresh" commonplace.

The majority of the United States' supplies of almonds, avocados, lentils, dates, figs, grapes, lemons, limes, olives, oranges, peaches, plums, tomatoes, walnuts and turkeys as well as much of its dairy products come from California.

The variety of agricultural products is phenomenal and until one takes a serious look at California's sophisticated agricultural industry there is no way to understand how far-reaching it is.

The culinary traditions of California carry a certain simplicity and purity that is true to fresh flavors and blends of fresh ingredients. California cuisine is unique and is a distinct, American regional cuisine. When comparisons are made, many compare it to Mediterranean or Spanish/Mexican or Pacific Rim cuisines, but that's only because they might find it so difficult to describe California's rich food heritage and diversity.

California's food traditions and flavors are as diverse as its people and as unique as its coastal harbors, mountain ranges, deserts and inland plains. It has the highest and lowest points in the contiguous 48 United States with Mt. Whitney at 14,495 feet above sea level and Bad Water in Death Valley at 282 feet below sea level. Its food traditions and diversity at every level are just as astounding and amazing. California, like its food, terrain and people are almost indescribable.

A Short History of California

California's first inhabitants lived more than 10,000 years ago and the diversity of peoples was as strong then as it is today. There were more than 70 culturally distinct tribes of American Indians living primarily on the coast and around rivers. They hunted sea mammals, fished and gathered shellfish. The tribes located more inland gathered berries, nuts and acorns.

Political and social cultures mixed over time and modern-day history shows the strongest European influences came from the Spanish starting in 1542. Juan Rodriguez Cabrillo was a Portuguese explorer who sailed for Spain to find and to claim new lands.

Spanish explorers Hernando Cortez and Ortuno Ximenez gave California its name. The golden fields of yellow poppies that bloom in the spring probably reminded them of the gold-laden island ruled by a queen named Califia made popular in the novel, *Las Sergas de Esplandian*, by Garcia Ordonez de Montalvo in 1510. Spanish explorers originally thought that California was an island and old maps reflect this idea.

Almost 40 years later Francis Drake also explored the California coast and claimed some of it for Britain. Spanish explorers brought missionaries who had great influence on the territory, notably Father Junipero Serra. They set up a vast mission system along the coast and began some of the agricultural and cultural paths that Californians follow today.

The Spanish introduced almonds, apples, apricots, bananas, barley, beans, cherries, chick-peas, chilies, citrons, dates, figs, grapes, lemons, lentils, limes, maize, olives, nectarines, oranges, peaches, pears, plums, pomegranates, quinces, tomatias, walnuts, wheat, chickens, cows, donkeys, goats, horses, sheep and domesticated turkey.

The territory along the coast was called Alta California (upper California) beginning with the first mission at San Diego in

1769. When the English, Portuguese, Italians and Russians came to the area, their reports created more excitement about this new land.

Beginning in the 1820's, settlers came to Alta California as trails opened up over the rugged mountains and harsh deserts that separated the new territory from the eastern United States. The Old Spanish Trail, the California Trail and the Oregon Trail led settlers to places along the coast.

In 1821 the Mexican War of Independence with Spain gave Mexico the area called Alta California and it remained a remote part of Mexico. In the Mexican-American War of 1846, the California Republic was formed to fight against Mexico. The Republic was short-lived, however, when Commodore John Sloat of the United States Navy sailed into San Francisco Bay and began the military occupation.

Following the Treaty of Guadalupe Hidalgo (1848) that ended the Mexican-American War, the territory which included what is today California, Arizona, Nevada, Utah and Colorado was given to the U.S. and Baja California remained in the hands of Mexico. It wasn't until 1850 that California became a state.

The Gold Rush of 1848, the completion of the First Transcontinental Railroad in 1869 and the construction of major highways like Route 66 in the early 20th century made it easier for the migration of people from the east to the west. People viewed the entire state as a gold mine rich with agricultural and economic opportunities.

Today California has the seventh largest economy in the world. Los Angeles has the fourth largest economy compared to all the states in the U.S. Two of the ten most populous cities in the U.S. are Los Angeles and San Diego.

California is the largest producer of processed tomatoes in the world and the second largest producer of pistachios in the world. It accounts for 90% of wine production in the U.S., 99.5% of dates grown in the U.S. and more than 75% of strawberries grown in the U.S. Its agricultural products are known worldwide.

Map of California

- Eureka
- Redding
- Lake Tahoe
- ★ Sacramento
- Santa Rosa
- Yosemite NP
- San Francisco
- Sequoia & Kings Canyon NP
- Monterey/Salinas
- Fresno
- Death Valley NP
- Bakersfield
- Santa Barbara
- Oxnard/Ventura
- Joshua Tree NP
- Los Angeles
- Palm Springs
- NP = National Park
- San Diego

Dedication

With a mission of helping you bring family and friends to the table, Cookbook Resources strives to make family meals and entertaining friends simple, easy and delicious.

We recognize the importance of sharing meals as a means of building family bonds with memories and traditions that will be treasured for a lifetime. Mealtime is an opportunity to sit down with each other and share more than food.

This cookbook is dedicated with gratitude and respect for all those who show their love with homecooked meals, bringing family and friends to the table.

Contents

Appetizers and Snacks 11

Dips, Salsas, Finger Foods, Trail Mix

Beverages 37

Coffees, Tea, Smoothies, Punches

Breakfast, Brunch and Breads 45

Soups and Salads 53

Fruits, Veggies, Meats

Vegetables and Side Dishes 75

Main Dishes 97

Beef, Chicken, Pork, Seafood

Sweets 155

Cakes. Pies, Cookies, Desserts

California Food Festivals

Month	Festival Name	Place
January	Annual Mendocino Crab and Wine Days	Mendocino
	Holtville Rib Cook-Off Extravaganza	Holtville
	ZAP'S Annual Zinfandel Festival	San Francisco
February	Annual Celebrity Crab Festival	San Francisco
	Annual Santa Cruz Clam Chowder Festival	Santa Cruz
	Annual Winter and Food Festival	Sacramento
	Gold Coast Chocolate Festival	Ventura
	Holtville Carrot Festival	Holtville
	Napa Valley Mustard Festival	Napa Valley
	National Date Festival	Indio
	San Francisco Crab Festival	San Francisco
March	Paso Robles Zinfandel Festival	Paso Robles
April	Annual Petaluma Butter and Egg Day	Petaluma
	Annual Stanta Barbara County Vintners' Festival	Santa Barbara
	California Poppy Festival	Lancaster
	California Wine Festival	San Diego
	International Beer Festival	San Francisco
	Placer County Strawberry Festival	Roseville
	Stockton Asparagus Festival	Stockton
	World Beer Cup	San Diego
May	Artichoke Festival	Castroville
	California Festival of Beers	Avila Beach
	California Strawberry Festival	Oxnard
	Food & Wine Festival	Newport Beach
	Mayfaire Homebrew Festival	Ventura
	San Francisco Oyster-Beer Festival	San Francisco
	Southern California Homebrewer's Festival	Temecula
	Uncorked: The San Francisco Wine Festival	San Francisco
	West Coast Brew Festival	Sacramento
June	Annual Monterey Wine Festival	Monterey
	Annual Pinot Days	San Francisco

California Food Festivals

Month	Festival Name	Place
June	North Beach Festival	San Francisco
	Ojai Wine Festival	Ojai
	Perris Potato Festival	Perris
	Sushi and Sake Festival	Long Beach
	Zinfandel Madness	Napa
July	Annual Gilroy Garlic Festival	Gilroy
	Annual Oxnard Salsa Festival	Oxnard
	California Peach Festival	Marysville
	California Wine Festival	Santa Barbara
August	Annual Bodega Bay Seafood Festival	Bodega
	Annual Tomato Festival	Fairfield
	Long Beach Crab Festival	Long Beach
	Monterey Bay Strawberry Festival	Watsonville
	San Diego Fruit Festival	San Diego
	Tofu Festival	Los Angeles
September	Annual Ghirardelli Square Chocolate Festival	San Francisco
	Annual NatureSweet Carmel Tomato Festival	Carmel
	Annual Redondo Beach Lobster Festival	Redondo Beach
	Festival of the Fruit	Orange County
	Italian Family Festival	San Jose
	Julian Grap Stomp Festival	Julian
	Pittsburg Seafood Festival	Pittsburg
	Port of Los Angeles Lobster Festival	San Pedro
October	Annual California Avocado Festival	Carpinteria
	Annual Los Angeles International Tamale Festival	Los Angeles
	Loose Goose Wine Festival	Santa Clarita Valley
	Oakhurst Fall Chocolate & Wine Festival	Oakhurst
November	Harvest Wine Celebration	Temecula
	San Diego Bay Wine and Food Festival	San Diego
December	Indio International Tamale Festival	Indio

California National Parks

Name	Location
Alcatraz Island (Golden Gate National Recreation Area)	San Francisco
Cabrillo National Monument	San Diego,
California National Historic Trail	Various States
Channel Islands National Park	Ventura
Death Valley National Park	Death Valley
Devils Postpile National Monument	Mammoth Lakes
Eugene O'Neill National Historic Site	Danville
Fort Point National Historic Site	Presidio of San Francisco
Golden Gate National Recreation Area	San Francisco
John Muir National Historic Site	Martinez
Joshua Tree National Park	Twentynine Palms
Juan Bautista de Anza National Historic Trail	Nogales, Arizona to San Francisco,
Kings Canyon National Park	Tulare and Fresno counties
Lassen Volcanic National Park	Mineral
Lava Beds National Monument	Tulelake
Manzanar National Historic Site	Independence
Mojave National Preserve	Barstow
Muir Woods National Monument	Mill Valley
Old Spanish National Historic Trail	Various StatesT
Pinnacles National Monument	Paicines
Point Reyes National Seashore	Point Reyes
Pony Express National Historic Trail	Various States
Port Chicago Naval Magazine National Memorial	Concord Naval Weapons Station
Presidio of San Francisco (Golden Gate NRA)	San Francisco
Redwood National and State Parks	Del Norte and Humboldt counties
Rosie the Riveter WWII Home Front Nat'l Historical Park	Richmond
San Francisco Maritime National Historical Park	San Francisco
Santa Monica Mountains National Recreation Area	Thousand Oaks
Sequoia National Park	Tulare and Fresno counties
Whiskeytown National Recreation Area	Whiskeytown
Yosemite National Park	the Sierra Nevada

Appetizers and Snacks

Dips
Salsas
Finger Foods
Trail Mix

Official Motto of California
"Eureka!"
(I have found it!)

Official Slogan of California
"Find Yourself Here"

Curry Lover's Veggie Dip

1 cup mayonnaise
½ cup sour cream
1 teaspoon curry powder
¼ teaspoon hot sauce
1 teaspoon lemon juice
Paprika
Raw vegetables

- Combine all ingredients except paprika and vegetables in bowl and mix until they blend well.

- Sprinkle a little paprika for color. Cover and refrigerate. Serve with raw vegetables. Yields 1½ cups.

Kahlua Fruit Dip

1 (8 ounce) package cream cheese, softened
1 (8 ounce) carton whipped topping
⅔ cup packed brown sugar
⅓ cup Kahlua® liqueur
1 (8 ounce) carton sour cream
Fresh fruit

- Whip cream cheese in bowl until creamy and fold in whipped topping.

- Add brown sugar, Kahlua® and sour cream and mix well.

- Refrigerate for 24 hours before serving with fresh fruit. Yields 3 cups.

Mount Whitney which borders Sequoia National Park east of Fresno, California is 14,495 feet high and is the highest peak in the contiguous 48 United States. Wilderness permits are required to reach the summit by way of Mount Whitney Trail.

Gilroy Roasted Garlic Dip

4 - 5 whole garlic cloves with peels
Olive oil
2 (8 ounce) packages cream cheese, softened
¾ cup mayonnaise
1 (7 - 9 ounce) jar sweet roasted red peppers, drained,
    coarsely chopped
1 bunch fresh green onions with tops, chopped
Red pepper or paprika
Chips

- Preheat oven to 400°.

- Lightly brush outside of garlic cloves with a little oil and place in shallow baking pan. Heat for about 10 minutes and cool. Press roasted garlic out of cloves.

- Beat cream cheese and mayonnaise in bowl until creamy. Add roasted garlic, roasted peppers and green onions and mix well. (Roasted peppers are great in this recipe, but if you want it a little spicy, add several drops of hot sauce.)

- Sprinkle with red pepper or paprika and serve with chips. Yields 3½ cups.

The Gilroy Garlic Festival in Gilroy, California serves more than two tons of fresh garlic prepared in every conceivable way.

Ginger Fruit Dip

1 (3 ounce) package cream cheese, softened
1 (7 ounce) jar marshmallow creme
½ cup mayonnaise
1 teaspoon ground ginger
1 teaspoon grated orange peel
Fresh fruit sticks

- Beat cream cheese in bowl on medium speed until smooth. Add marshmallow creme, mayonnaise, ginger and orange peel, and stir until smooth.

- Serve with fresh fruit sticks. Yields 1½ cups.

California Clam Dip

1 (1 ounce) packet onion soup mix
2 (8 ounce) cartons sour cream
1 (7 ounce) can minced clams, drained
3 tablespoons chili sauce
1 tablespoon lemon juice
Assorted crackers

- Combine onion soup mix and sour cream in bowl and mix well.

- Add clams, chili sauce and lemon juice.

- Refrigerate. Serve with assorted crackers. Yields 2 cups.

"The greatest service which can be rendered any country is to add a useful plant to its culture." —Thomas Jefferson, 1813

California Growers' Guacamole

4 – 5 ripe California avocados
4 – 5 cloves garlic, minced
1 cup crumbled gorgonzola or goat cheese
½ cup minced cilantro
¼ cup minced pistachios, toasted
½ teaspoon crushed peppercorns

- Peel and coarsely mash avocados in bowl, but leave some bite-sized pieces in bowl. Add remaining ingredients and serve immediately. Yields about 1 pint.

So-Cal Guacamole

4 ripe avocados
2 Anaheim chilies, seeded, minced
3 tablespoons lime juice
2 tablespoons tomatillo salsa
1 clove garlic, minced
¼ cup minced cilantro
Hot pepper sauce

- Peel and coarsely mash avocados, but leave some bite-sized pieces. Mix all ingredients in bowl.

- Add a little salt, pepper and a little hot sauce and serve immediately. Yields about 1 pint.

The annual Avocado Festival is held in Fallbrook which claims the title of Avocado Capital of the World. More avocados are grown in California than in any other state.

Capitola Ceviche

1 pound halibut, cut in ½-inch pieces
12 – 15 lemons or 1 (15 ounce) bottle lemon or lime juice
4 – 6 large tomatoes, seeded, chopped
2 large green bell peppers, seeded, minced
4 – 6 green onions with tops, minced
5 – 6 green chile peppers or jalapenos, seeded, chopped
½ cup olive oil
1 cup ketchup
Pinch of oregano

- Marinate halibut in lemon or lime juice for at least 4 hours. (The action of the lemon or lime juice "cooks" fish and turns it to an opaque color.)

- Add tomatoes, bell peppers, green onions, green chilies (enough for desired "heat"), oil, ketchup and oregano.

- Refrigerate for several hours or overnight and serve as appetizer. Yields 2 pints.

California's early farmers and ranchers were Spanish missionaries, followed by Mexicans, Japanese, Portuguese, Dutch and other Europeans as well as Chinese and Russians.

Valley Beans-Avocado Stack

Great fun to eat and a pretty picture too.

1 (15 ounce) can refried beans
½ cup sour cream
⅓ cup mayonnaise
3 avocados
1 lemon
2 tomatoes, diced
4 green onions with tops, chopped
2 (4 ounce) cans diced green chilies
1 clove garlic, minced
1 (10 ounce) jar hot salsa
1 (8 ounce) package shredded Monterey Jack cheese
Chips or crackers

- Combine refried beans, sour cream and mayonnaise in blender and process. Peel, remove seeds and mash avocados in small bowl. Squeeze juice of lemon over avocados and mix thoroughly.

- Add tomatoes, green onions, green chilies and garlic to avocados and stir well. Spoon refried bean layer in 9-inch glass pie pan or make 9-inch circle in middle of large platter.

- Spread avocados evenly over top of beans. Pour hot salsa evenly over avocados and top with cheese. Serve with chips or crackers. Yields 2 pints.

San Francisco Bay is the largest landlocked harbor in the world.

Fresh Tomato Salsa

4 medium tomatoes, diced
2 - 4 green onions with tops, diced
1 - 2 jalapeno peppers
½ cup snipped cilantro leaves
Juice of 1 small lime
1 teaspoon sugar

- Dice tomatoes and onions in large bowl to save juices.

- Wash jalapenos, remove stems and seeds and dry with paper towels. Dice jalapenos and add to tomato-onion mixture.

- Combine with all other ingredients and 1 teaspoon salt and refrigerate for about 15 to 20 minutes.

- Remove from refrigerator and taste. If tomatoes are too tart, add a little sugar to cut tartness. Refrigerate for about 30 minutes more to blend flavors and serve. Yields 1½ cups.

Harmony Tomato Salsa

3 large tomatoes, peeled, seeded, chopped
3 - 4 fresh Anaheim green chilies, roasted, seeded, minced
2 cloves garlic, minced
1 jalapeno chile, seeded, minced
1 bunch green onions with tops, minced
1 bunch fresh cilantro, snipped
½ teaspoon cumin
Chips

- Mix all ingredients (except chips) and a little salt and pepper in large bowl and refrigerate for several hours for flavors to blend.

- Serve in small bowls with chips or over fish or vegetables. Yields 2 cups.

Sweet Pepper-Jicama Salsa

5 tomatoes, seeded, chopped
1 bunch green onions with tops, chopped
2 jicama, peeled, chopped
1 red bell pepper, seeded, chopped
1 yellow bell pepper, seeded, chopped
1 green bell pepper, seeded, chopped
1 cucumber, peeled, chopped
2 bunches fresh cilantro, snipped
3 cloves garlic, minced
¼ cup olive oil
¼ cup balsamic vinegar
¼ cup lime juice
1 – 2 teaspoon(s) cayenne pepper
1 tablespoon cumin

- Mix tomatoes, onions, jicama, bell peppers and cucumber in large bowl and toss gently.

- In separate bowl, mix cilantro, garlic, oil, vinegar, lime juice, cayenne pepper and cumin and blend well.

- Pour over vegetables and toss to coat with dressing. Store in closed container in refrigerator and toss occasionally. Yields 1½ pints.

There is less than six hours time from when tomatoes are picked to when they are processed and in a can.

California tomato season is between June and November with the peak season running from July to September. During the peak season harvesters work 24 hours a day.

Magic Mango Salsa

This goes great with grilled fish or chicken.

2 ripe mangoes, peeled, chopped
2 tomatoes, seeded, chopped
1 cucumber, seeded, chopped
1 green onion with tops, chopped
1 fresh jalapeno pepper, seeded, veined, chopped
¼ cup snipped fresh cilantro
1 tablespoon lime juice

- Mix all ingredients in bowl or container with lid. Refrigerate for several hours before serving.

- Use slotted spoon to serve. Yields 2 cups.

TIP: *Make sure you get ripe mangoes and the fruit is sweet next to its seed before adding it to the salsa.*

The California condor is celebrated on California's state quarter to highlight the successful repopulation of the almost extinct bird. The California condor has a wingspan of more than nine feet.

Roasted Chile Salsa

4 – 5 poblano chilies
3 mild jalapeno peppers
2 red bell peppers
2 yellow bell peppers
1 large sweet onion, minced
4 – 5 cloves garlic, minced
¼ cup extra virgin olive oil
¼ cup fresh lime juice
¼ cup snipped cilantro or fresh oregano
Cracked black pepper

- To roast poblano chilies, hold them over open flame of gas burner or broil them in oven until outside turns dark brown on all sides. (Be careful not to burn holes through skin.)

- Place chilies in resealable plastic bag, seal and allow to sweat for about 15 to 20 minutes so skin will slide off easily. Remove skins and slice through length of chile on one side. Remove seeds, but leave veins intact.

- Follow same roasting procedure for jalapenos and bell peppers. Remove seeds and veins. Chop or mince all peppers.

- Mix all remaining ingredients plus a little salt in bowl and serve with fish or chicken. Yields 1 pint.

Chula Vista Stuffed Jalapenos

1 pound fresh jalapeno peppers
1 (8 ounce) package cream cheese, softened
2 eggs, hard-boiled, mashed
½ teaspoon garlic salt
¼ cup finely chopped pecans
1 (2 ounce) can chopped pimentos, drained
Mayonnaise
Paprika

- Halve peppers lengthwise and remove seeds and veins.

- Beat cream cheese with mashed eggs, garlic salt, pecans, pimentos and a little salt in bowl.

- Add enough mayonnaise to make a paste consistency.

- Fill peppers and mound stuffing slightly. Sprinkle tops with paprika. Serves 10.

The hottest and driest places in the U.S. are in Death Valley, located in the southeastern part of the state.

Tuna-Stuffed Anaheim Chilies

6 - 8 large Anaheim chilies
1 (3 ounce) package cream cheese, softened
¼ cup mayonnaise
1 (7 ounce) can white tuna in water, drained
2 tablespoons lemon juice
¼ cup chopped walnuts
Olive oil

- Slice whole chilies in half, remove seeds, drain and soak in ice water.

- Beat cream cheese, mayonnaise, tuna, lemon juice and walnuts in bowl and mix well. Rub each chile half with a little oil and stuff each half with cream cheese filling. Serves 8.

TIP: It is a good idea to handle all peppers and chilies with gloves or wash hands thoroughly with soap and water after handling.

Stompin' Good Jalapeno Squares

2 (4 ounce) cans jalapeno peppers, seeded, chopped
1 pound bacon, fried, crumbled
1 (12 ounce) package shredded Mexican 4-cheese blend
1 (4 ounce) can sliced mushroom stems and pieces, drained
10 eggs, well beaten

- Preheat oven to 325°.

- Place jalapenos in sprayed 9 x 13-inch baking dish.

- Sprinkle bacon pieces, cheese and mushrooms in layers. Pour beaten eggs over top.

- Cook for about 25 to 30 minutes or until center is firm.

- Let stand for 15 minutes before slicing. Cut into squares and serve hot. Serves 8.

TIP: If you want a mild "hot", just use 1 can jalapenos.

Green Chile Squares

2 cups chopped green chilies
1 (8 ounce) package shredded sharp cheddar cheese
8 eggs, beaten
½ cup half-and-half cream

- Preheat oven to 350°.

- Place green chilies in sprayed 9 x 13-inch baking pan and cover with cheese.

- Combine eggs, a little salt and pepper and half-and-half cream in bowl. Pour over chilies and cheese.

- Bake for 30 minutes. Let stand at room temperature for a few minutes before cutting into squares. Serves 6.

A typical tomato truck holds 50,000 pounds of tomatoes which is about 300,000 tomatoes.

The Spanish colonists in California introduced almonds, apples, apricots, bananas, barley, beans, cherries, chick-peas, chilies, citrons, dates, figs, grapes, lemons, lentils, limes, maize, olives, nectarines, oranges, peaches, pears, plums, pomegranates, quinces, tomatias, walnuts, wheat, chickens, cows, donkeys, goats, horses, sheep and domesticated turkey. Spanish colonists also introduced saffron, olive oil and anise.

Garlic-Stuffed Mushrooms

1 tablespoon extra-virgin olive oil
2 tablespoons butter
¾ cup Italian breadcrumbs
3 cloves garlic, peeled, minced
¼ teaspoon oregano
½ teaspoon seasoned salt
¼ teaspoon cracked black pepper
18 large mushrooms, stems removed

- Preheat oven to 400°.

- Heat olive oil and butter in skillet over medium heat. Add breadcrumbs, stir to coat and cook for about 5 minutes.

- Add garlic, oregano, seasoned salt and fresh ground black pepper and saute until garlic is translucent.

- Stuff each mushroom with breadcrumb mixture and place in sprayed 9 x 13-inch baking pan. Bake for 20 minutes or until mushrooms are tender. Serve hot or at room temperature. Serves 10 to 12.

California-Style Pizza

1 tablespoon olive oil
2 cloves garlic, peeled, minced, divided
2 fresh green onions, minced
1 (12 inch) prepared pizza crust
1 (10 ounce) package frozen chopped spinach, thawed
1½ cups shredded mozzarella cheese
8 – 10 grape or cherry tomatoes, halved
1 (4 ounce) can sliced black olives, drained
1 (10 ounce) can green olives, drained, sliced, divided
1 (4 ounce) package crumbled feta cheese

- Preheat oven to 400°.

- Mix oil, 1 clove garlic and green onions in small, microwave-safe bowl and microwave on HIGH for 30 seconds. Prepare pizza crust by rubbing garlic mixture over surface of crust.

- Squeeze spinach between paper towels to completely remove excess moisture. Spread spinach evenly over crust. Sprinkle mozzarella cheese evenly over spinach.

- Add tomato halves, black olives and about half of green olives evenly over cheese. Sprinkle with a little salt and pepper and top with feta cheese.

- Bake for about 10 minutes or until cheese melts and crust is golden brown. Let stand 5 minutes before cutting into slices to serve. Serves 2 to 4.

Tomatoes that are loaded onto tomato trucks in bulk have been specially bred to have a thicker skin and to be able to withstand loading and shipping without much damage.

Cheesy Caesar Pizza

1 (12 inch) prepared Italian pizza crust
1 (8 ounce) package shredded mozzarella cheese
1 (6 ounce) package cooked chicken breast strips
2 cups shredded lettuce
3 fresh green onions, sliced
¾ cup shredded cheddar-colby cheese
½ (8 ounce) bottle Caesar dressing

- Preheat oven to 400°.

- Top pizza crust with mozzarella cheese and bake for 5 minutes or until cheese melts.

- Combine chicken strips, lettuce, green onions and cheese in bowl. Pour about half of Caesar dressing over salad and toss.

- Top hot pizza with salad and cut into wedges. Serve immediately. Serves 4 to 6.

Chef Caesar Cardini of Caesar's Palace, a popular restaurant in Tijuana, Mexico created Caesar Salad with just a few remaining ingredients in his kitchen one night in the 1920's.

He put together romaine lettuce, olive oil, parmesan cheese and a few eggs right beside the table. It was so popular with the guests that they called the dish Caesar's Salad.

Roasted-Garlic Snacker

Olive oil
5 - 6 garlic cloves, peeled
2 (8 ounce) packages cream cheese, softened
¾ cup mayonnaise
1 (9 ounce) jar roasted sweet red peppers, drained,
    coarsely chopped
1 bunch fresh green onions with tops, chopped
Red pepper flakes
Chips or crackers

- Preheat oven to 350°.

- Lightly rub a little oil on outside of each garlic clove and place in sprayed, shallow baking pan. Heat for about 10 minutes and cool.

- Press roasted garlic from outer skins. Beat cream cheese and mayonnaise in bowl and stir in garlic, red peppers and onions and mix well.

- Sprinkle with red pepper flakes and serve with chips or crackers. Serves 4 to 6.

TIP: *Roasted red peppers can be found in jars at the local grocery store. They are not hot, but flavorful. If you would like a little spicier dip, add several drops of hot sauce or red pepper flakes.*

Garlic is a member of the onion family and has a pungent, spicy flavor that softens and becomes sweeter after it's cooked. Garlic is sold in bulbs or heads which can be divided into small sections called cloves.

Gilroy's Best Baked Garlic

2 large heads elephant garlic or 4 - 6 regular heads garlic
½ cup chicken stock
½ cup white wine
2 tablespoons unsalted butter, melted
Italian bread, sliced

- Preheat oven to 300°.

- Cut about ½ inch off top of garlic to expose cloves, remove papery skin and discard. Place in small baking dish and pour chicken stock and wine to almost cover garlic.

- Pour melted butter into heads and sprinkle with a little salt and pepper.

- Cover and bake until tender, about 1 hour Uncover.

- Remove garlic, break into cloves and squeeze garlic from each. Spread on Italian bread and serve with sauce from baking dish for dipping. Yields 1 cup.

Grilled Tomato-Basil Tortillas

Extra-virgin olive oil
6 (6 inch) corn or flour tortillas
2 large tomatoes, seeded, diced, drained
1 bunch green onions with tops, chopped
¼ cup snipped basil leaves
1 cup shredded mozzarella cheese

- Spread light coating of olive oil on both sides of tortilla. Spread tomatoes, onions and basil on top of each tortilla. Cover with cheese.

- Place over low heat on charcoal or gas grill and cook until cheese melts. Break into smaller pieces or serve whole. Serves 4 to 6.

Brie Baked with Roasted Garlic and Sun-Dried Tomatoes

1 large whole head garlic
Extra-virgin olive oil
Sprigs of rosemary
1 (12 ounce) round brie cheese
½ - ¾ cup sun-dried tomatoes in oil, drained, chopped
⅓ cup pine nuts
⅓ cup snipped fresh basil leaves
Crostini

- Preheat oven to 350°.

- Cut about ¼ inch from pointed end of garlic head to expose cloves inside. Place cut end up in foil bowl formed around garlic head.

- Drizzle a little olive oil on top of garlic and drop 2 rosemary sprigs on top. Close foil package loosely. Bake for 45 minutes or until cloves of garlic are tender.

- When garlic cools enough to touch, squeeze garlic out of cloves into small bowl. Stir and spread over round of brie. Arrange tomatoes and pine nuts on top.

- Bake brie for about 15 minutes or until creamy on the inside. Cover top with foil if it begins to brown too much.

- Sprinkle top with basil and serve immediately with crostini or crackers. Serves 8 to 12.

Tomatoes grown for processing are picked ripe and red. Fresh market tomatoes are picked green.

Yucca Quesadillas with Goat Cheese and Nopalitos

Nopalitos, the small pads of prickly pear cactus, add a wonderful, complementary flavor to the goat cheese.

6 Anaheim green chilies, roasted, peeled, seeded
6 (6 inch) flour tortillas
1 (16 ounce) carton goat cheese
1 (15 ounce) jar nopalitos, drained well
2 avocados, sliced

- Cut chilies into strips. Lay 1 tortilla in large skillet and sprinkle one-third goat cheese to within ½ inch of edge. Add one-third nopalitos, one-third avocados and one-third chilies over cheese and top with another tortilla. Repeat process with remaining tortillas.

- Heat until cheese begins to melt or tortilla browns slightly. Turn to other side and heat until cheese melts. Cut into wedges and serve immediately. Serves 3 to 6.

Some of the gnarled bristlecone pine trees located in Inyo National Forest are thought to be over 4,600 years old.

Fried-Baked Japanese Wings

5 pounds chicken wings
2 eggs, beaten
2 cups flour
Canola oil
2 cups sugar
1 cup white vinegar
⅓ cup soy sauce
1 teaspoon garlic powder

- Preheat oven to 350°.

- Cut wings into 2 pieces, discard end piece and season rest with a little salt and pepper. Dip wings in eggs and dredge through flour.

- Heat oil in large skillet and fry wings until they are golden brown. Drain on paper towels and arrange in 9 x 13-inch baking pan.

- Mix sugar, vinegar, soy sauce, garlic powder and ½ teaspoon salt in bowl and pour over wings. Bake for 30 to 35 minutes and baste frequently in sauce. Serves 8 to 10.

Devil's Canyon Cooked-Up Granola

2 cups old-fashioned oats
1 tablespoon canola oil
⅓ cup packed brown sugar
⅓ cup butter
2 tablespoons honey
⅓ cup dried cranberries
½ cup sliced almonds

- Place oats in skillet with hot oil and cook over medium heat until oats begin to brown and crisp. Drain and transfer oats to baking sheet.

- Mix brown sugar, butter and honey in same skillet and cook over medium heat, stirring constantly, until bubbly.

- Remove from heat and pour in oats. Mix well and return all ingredients to baking sheet to cool. Add cranberries and almonds to mixture and store in airtight container. Serves 8.

TIP: Add your favorite dried fruits and nuts to the mixture for your own special blend of flavors.

One of California's nicknames is "The Land of Milk and Honey". California has always been associated with opportunities and plenty and the reference to the land of milk and honey (the promised land) comes from the Bible.

Happy Trails Granola

6 cups old-fashioned oats
1½ cups unsweetened coconut
1 cup sliced almonds or pistachios
½ cup crushed wheat germ
½ cup sunflower seeds
½ cup sesame seeds
⅔ cup honey
½ cup canola oil
1 tablespoon vanilla
2 teaspoons ground cinnamon
1 teaspoon ground nutmeg
1 cup raisins

- Preheat oven to 350°.

- Mix oats, coconut, almonds, wheat germ, sunflower seeds and sesame seeds in 9 x 13-inch baking pan.

- Mix honey, oil, vanilla, cinnamon and nutmeg in bowl and pour over granola mix. Stir well to coat all pieces with honey mixture.

- Bake for about 30 minutes. Cool mixture and add raisins. Store in airtight container. Serves 8 to 10.

California's "Dancing Raisins" were created by the California Raisin Industry marketing group to increase awareness of and consumption of raisins and were introduced in 1984.

Granola Bars

7 cups old-fashioned oats
½ cup canola oil
¾ cup honey
¾ cup packed brown sugar
1 tablespoon vanilla
1 teaspoon ground cinnamon
1½ cups chopped walnuts

- Preheat oven to 375°.

- Toss oats, oil and ½ teaspoon salt in large bowl. Spread out over cookie sheet, bake and stir often for 20 to 25 minutes or until pale gold in color.

- Cook honey and brown sugar in small saucepan over medium heat, stirring frequently, until sugar dissolves, about 5 minutes. Stir in vanilla and cinnamon and set aside.

- Remove oats from oven and lower oven heat to 300°. Transfer baked oats to large bowl and toss with honey mixture until evenly coated. Stir in walnuts.

- Line 12 x 18-inch cookie sheet with sprayed foil. Spread oat mixture out on cookie sheet, then pack tightly into even layer using metal spatula.

- Bake for 35 to 40 minutes. Let cool for about 15 minutes and cut into 2 x 3-inch bars. Yields 36 bars.

Mixed Fruit-Nut Granola

This is a basic granola recipe in which you choose the fruit and nuts to make your own special snack.

1½ **cups old-fashioned oats**
½ **cup coarsely chopped nuts**
2 **tablespoons butter**
2 **tablespoons light brown sugar**
1 **tablespoon honey**
½ **teaspoon ground cinnamon**
¼ **cup chopped dried fruit**

- Preheat oven to 350°.

- Spread oats and nuts on baking sheet. Bake for 10 to 15 minutes and shake every 3 or 4 minutes. Cool.

- Combine butter, brown sugar, honey and cinnamon in 1-quart saucepan over medium heat. Cook and stir until butter melts.

- Drizzle evenly over oat mixture. Cool and combine dried fruit with oat mixture in large bowl. Store in airtight container. Serves 10.

Beverages

Coffees
Teas
Smoothies
Punches

Official Animal of California:
California Grizzly Bear

Official Bird of California:
California Valley Quail

Cafe Latte

According to wikipedia.com, "cafe latte" was first invented at the Caffe Mediterranean in Berkeley, California in 1959. When the owner served his strong espresso-style coffee, patrons asked for milk. Eventually the drink evolved to the same strong brew with enough steamed milk for Americans' taste.

⅔ cup milk, steamed
⅓ cup brewed espresso

- Pour steamed milk into espresso and leave about ¼ inch foam on top. Serves 1.

Note: Cappuccino has ⅓ cup espresso, ⅓ cup steamed milk and ⅓ cup foam on top.

Easy Breakfast Cappuccino

1 packet cappuccino instant breakfast nutritional energy drink
¾ cup milk
⅛ teaspoon ground cinnamon
⅛ teaspoon ground cardamom
½ teaspoon vanilla or almond flavoring

- Mix all ingredients in tall glass and add ice. Serves 1.

Smooth Mocha Mudslide

2 cups cafe mocha liquid coffee creamer
2 tablespoons French roast instant coffee granules
2 cups vanilla ice cream or frozen yogurt

• Mix creamer and coffee in blender. Add ice cream and about
  3 to 4 cups ice and blend until smooth. Serve cold.
  Serves 3 to 4.

Black Forest Buzz

1 cup hot brewed coffee
2 tablespoons chocolate syrup
1 tablespoon maraschino cherry juice

• Pour coffee into coffee mug, add chocolate syrup and cherry
  juice and stir well. Serve hot. Serves 1.

Japanese Green Tea

Green tea leaves

• The best pot for brewing tea is the Japanese teapot
  called kyusu. The best tea cups have no handles and are
  called yunomi.

• Pour boiling water into teapot and cool to best temperature:
  160° for sencha and macha green tea, 110° for gyukuro
  green tea.

• Pour hot water over tea leaves, cover and brew sencha for
  about 1 minute. Decide best times for your tastes.

Create-Your-Own Smoothies

Here's a basic formula. You choose the ingredients and make your favorite concoctions.

2 cups liquid:	apple juice, orange juice, milk
½ – 1 cup fresh fruit slices:	peach, apricot, pears, strawberries, raspberries, blueberries
Creamy ingredient:	1 banana
Sweetener:	1 teaspoon honey
Calcium source:	¼ cup yogurt, frozen yogurt
Flavorings:	Vanilla, almond extract, cinnamon, nutmeg

- Combine all ingredients in bowl and pour into blender and process until smooth. Pour into tall glass with ice or plain.

- For an icy texture, add ice to the blender while processing. Serves 2.

Banana Split Float Smoothie

2 ripe bananas, mashed
3 cups milk
1 (10 ounce) package frozen sweetened strawberries, thawed
1½ pints chocolate ice cream, divided

- Place bananas in blender and add milk, strawberries and ½ pint chocolate ice cream.

- Process just until they blend.

- Pour into tall, chilled glasses and top each with scoop of chocolate ice cream. Serves 3.

Seaside Surf Smoothie

1½ heaping cups peeled, seeded ripe papaya
1 very ripe large banana
1½ heaping cups ripe cantaloupe, cut into chunks
1 (6 ounce) carton coconut cream pie yogurt
¼ cup milk

- Cut papaya into chunks. Place all ingredients in blender and process until smooth.

- Pour into glasses and serve immediately. Serves 2 to 4.

Banana-Mango Smoothie

1 cup peeled, cubed ripe mango
1 ripe banana, sliced
⅔ cup milk
1 teaspoon honey
¼ teaspoon vanilla

- Arrange mango cubes in single layer on baking sheet and freeze for about 1 hour or until firm.

- Combine frozen mango, banana, milk, honey and vanilla in blender and process until smooth. Serves 1.

California fruit crops include apples, apricots, avocados, boysenberries, raspberries, strawberries, grapes, lemons, oranges, tangerines, cherries, dates, figs, grapes, kiwifruit, nectarines, olives, peaches, pears and plums. California nut crops include almonds, pecans, pistachios and walnuts.

Go-Grapeberry Smoothie

2 pink grapefruit
1 cup chopped, ripe mango
1 medium banana
1 (8 ounce) carton strawberry–banana yogurt
2 tablespoons honey
½ teaspoon white vanilla

- Slice grapefruit into halves and squeeze enough fresh juice to equal 1⅓ cups.

- Pour juice into blender and add mango, banana, yogurt, honey, vanilla and about ½ cup ice.

- Blend and process several times. Add additional ½ cup ice and process until smooth. Serves 4 to 6.

James Marshall and his crew were building a sawmill for John Sutter on the American River at Coloma, California. On January 24, 1848, Marshall found a few nuggets of gold and the California Gold Rush spread across the United States.

Berry Special Smoothie

1½ cups milk
1 (8 ounce) carton blueberry or strawberry yogurt
1 teaspoon instant lemonade mix
1 cup strawberries
1 cup blueberries

- Combine milk, yogurt and lemonade mix and whip slightly in blender. Add strawberries and blueberries and process until smooth. Serves 3 to 4.

Chocolate-Banana Smoothie

1 cup milk
1 banana
1 tablespoon chocolate syrup

- Combine all ingredients in blender and process with crushed ice until slushy. Serves 1.

TIP: For a creamier texture, substitute ice cream or frozen yogurt for milk.

California's official state insect is the California Dogface Butterfly.

Citrus Grove Punch

3 cups sugar
6 cups orange juice, chilled
6 cups grapefruit juice, chilled
1½ cups lime juice, chilled
1 (1 liter) bottle ginger ale, chilled

- Bring sugar and 2 cups water in saucepan to a boil and cook for 5 minutes.

- Cover and refrigerate until cool.

- Combine juices and sugar mixture in bowl and mix well.

- Just before serving, stir in ginger ale. Serve over ice. Serves 18 to 22.

Lime Cooler

1½ pints lime sherbet, divided
1 (6 ounce) can frozen limeade concentrate
3 cups milk
Lime slices

- Beat 1 pint lime sherbet in bowl and add limeade concentrate and milk. Stir until they blend well.

- Pour into 5 glasses and top each with small scoop of lime sherbet. Garnish with lime slices.

- Serve immediately. Serves 5.

Breakfast, Brunch and Breads

Official Fish of California
California Golden Trout

Official Marine Fish of California
Garibaldi

Official Marine Mammal of California
California Gray Whale

Breakfast Fruit Bowl

1 cup flavored or plain yogurt
1 tablespoon honey
½ cup granola cereal
2 cups fresh pear, peach or apricot slices

- Mix yogurt and honey with granola in bowl and top with fruit slices. Make as individual servings in bowls or mix together and serve. Serves 4.

Avocado-Stuffed Omelet

8 large eggs
½ cup milk
1 California avocado, seeded, peeled, diced
¾ cup shredded Monterey Jack cheese
¾ cup seeded, minced, drained tomatoes
½ cup minced green onions with tops

- Beat eggs with milk in bowl vigorously. Pour into large, sprayed skillet. Cook over low heat until eggs begin to firm up. Slide eggs around in skillet while cooking.

- Mix avocado, cheese, tomatoes and onions in bowl and spread over one-half of eggs. Use spatula to lift other half of eggs onto cheese mixture. Cook until firm on the inside and cheese melts. Serves 4 to 6.

John Muir emigrated from Scotland in 1849 at age 11. He made his home in the Yosemite Valley in 1868 at age 30. He published more than 300 articles and 10 books that touted his naturalist and conservationist philosophy. In 1890 Congress established Yosemite National Park. In 1892 John Muir helped found the Sierra Club and served as its president until his death in 1914.

Egg-Cheese Burritos

¼ cup (½ stick) butter
6 eggs, well beaten
3 tablespoons milk
4 green onions with tops, chopped
2 Anaheim green chilies, roasted, peeled, chopped
1 (8 ounce) package shredded Mexican 4-cheese blend
Flour tortillas
Salsa

- Melt butter in large omelet pan or skillet, beat eggs with milk and pour into skillet.

- Scramble eggs in skillet and stir constantly to keep eggs from sticking and burning.

- When eggs are almost firm, sprinkle onions, green chilies and cheese over eggs and stir.

- Remove from heat and scoop eggs into flour tortilla. Add salsa and roll tortilla. Serve immediately. Serves 4 to 6.

The United States Mint's 50-State Quarters Program released the quarter in honor of California in 2005. It depicts conservationist John Muir looking at Yosemite Valley's "Half Dome" granite headwall and a soaring California condor. Inscriptions on the coin include "California", "John Muir", "Yosemite Valley" and "1850", the year California became a state.

Banana-Pineapple Loaf

This is wonderful sliced, buttered and toasted for breakfast.

1 cup (2 sticks) butter, softened
1 cup sugar
4 eggs
1 cup mashed ripe bananas
4 cups sifted flour
2 teaspoons baking powder
1 teaspoon baking soda
1 (15 ounce) can crushed pineapple with juice
1 (7 ounce) can flaked coconut
1 cup chopped pecans

- Preheat oven to 350°.

- Cream butter and sugar in bowl, add eggs and mix well. Stir in bananas.

- In separate bowl, sift flour, baking powder, baking soda and ½ teaspoon salt and add to butter mixture. Fold in pineapple, coconut and pecans.

- Pour into 2 sprayed, floured 9 x 5-inch loaf pans. Bake for 1 hour 10 minutes. Bread is done when toothpick inserted in center comes out clean. Serves 12 to 16.

TIP: For lunch, spread cream cheese on slices of banana-pineapple bread, cut into thirds and serve as finger sandwiches. Removing the crusts makes the sandwiches nicer.

Zucchini-Pineapple Bread

3 eggs, beaten
2 cups sugar
1 cup canola oil
2 teaspoons vanilla
2 cups grated zucchini
3 cups flour
1 teaspoon baking soda
1 tablespoon ground cinnamon
½ teaspoon baking powder
1 cup chopped pecans
1 (8 ounce) can crushed pineapple, drained
1 (8 ounce) carton cream cheese, softened

- Preheat oven to 325°.

- Mix eggs, sugar, oil and vanilla in bowl and mix well.

- Add remaining ingredients except cream cheese. Add
  1 teaspoon salt, mix well and pour into 2 sprayed, floured
  9 x 5-inch loaf pans.

- Bake for 60 minutes or until toothpick inserted in center
  comes out clean. Cool for several minutes.

- To serve, slice and spread with cream cheese. Serves 12 to 16.

Sweet Apple Loaf

⅔ cup (1⅓ sticks) butter
2 cups sugar
4 eggs
2 cups applesauce
⅓ cup milk
1 tablespoon lemon juice
4 cups flour
1 teaspoon ground cinnamon
2 teaspoons baking powder
1 teaspoon baking soda
1½ cups chopped pecans
¾ cup chopped maraschino cherries, well drained

- Preheat oven to 325°.

- Cream butter, sugar and eggs in bowl and beat for several minutes

- Stir in applesauce, milk and lemon juice.

- In separate bowl, sift flour, cinnamon, baking powder, baking soda, and 1 teaspoon salt. Add to the first mixture and mix well. Fold in pecans and cherries.

- Pour into 3 sprayed, floured loaf pans and bake for 1 hour. Bread is done when toothpick inserted in center comes out clean. Set aside for 10 to 15 minutes, remove from pans and cool on rack. Serve toasted for breakfast or spread with cream cheese for lunch.

TIP: This freezes well.

While chuck wagon cooks were making sourdough bread at every stop along the trail from Texas and Oklahoma to markets in Kansas, Gold Rush prospectors or "49ers" were making the same sourdough bread daily. San Francisco is famous for sourdough bread today not only because it continues this culinary tradition traced back to the Gold Rush days in 1849 but because it's good!.

Sourdough Starter and Bread

Starter:

1 package yeast
2 cups flour

- Dissolve yeast in 2 cups warm water in glass bowl. Add flour and mix well. (Use only glass bowl for mixing and do NOT leave metal utensils in starter.)

- Place starter in warm place overnight. Next morning, cover container and refrigerate. Use only glass container to store starter. Refrigerate starter when not in use and keep covered.

- Every 5 days add and stir into starter:

 1 cup milk
 ¼ cup sugar
 1 cup flour

- Do not use starter on day it is "fed". Always keep at least 2 cups mixture in container. Starter may be fed more frequently than every 5 days.

TIP: This recipe for sourdough starter takes about three days, but from then on, all you have to do is replenish your starter as you use it. If you find someone who already has sourdough starter, you can get a "start" from them and save yourself three days.

Sourdough Bread:

2 cups flour
1 tablespoon baking powder
2 tablespoons sugar
1 egg
2 cups Sourdough Starter

- Preheat oven to 350°.

- Mix flour, baking powder, 1 teaspoon salt and sugar in bowl, add egg and starter and mix well. Pour into loaf pan and place in warm place. Allow to double in bulk.

- When ready to bake, preheat oven to 350°.

- Bake for 30 to 35 minutes. Yields 1 loaf.

Palms Presto Spread Bread

French bread
1½ cups shredded parmesan cheese
2 cloves garlic, minced
¾ cup mayonnaise

- Slice bread into 36 slices and place on baking sheet. Mix parmesan cheese, garlic and mayonnaise in bowl.

- Spread mixture over each slice of bread equally. Broil in oven until bread begins to brown, about 4 minutes.

- Serve with spreads and dips. Yields 36 small slices.

Spanish explorers Hernando Cortez and Ortuno Ximenez gave California its name. The golden fields of yellow poppies that bloom in the spring probably reminded them of the gold-laden island ruled by a queen named Califia made popular in the novel, Las Sergas de Esplandian, *by Garcia Ordonez de Montalvo in 1510. Spanish explorers originally thought that California was an island and old maps reflect this idea.*

Soups
and Salads

Fruits
Veggies
Meats

Official Flower of California:
Golden Poppy

Official Colors of California :
Blue and Gold

Official Gemstone of California:
Benitoite

Pacific Grove Strawberry Soup

1½ cups fresh strawberries
1 cup orange juice
¼ cup honey
½ cup sour cream
½ cup white wine

- Combine all ingredients in blender and process until smooth.

- Chill thoroughly. Stir before serving. Serves 2.

Rancho Avocado-Cream Soup

4 ripe avocados, peeled, diced, divided
1½ cups whipping cream, divided
2 (14 ounce) cans chicken broth
¼ cup dry sherry

- Process half of avocados and half of cream in blender. Repeat with remaining avocados and cream.

- Bring chicken broth to a boil in saucepan, reduce heat and stir in avocado puree. Add 1 teaspoon salt and sherry and chill thoroughly. Serves 6.

The California Strawberry Festival is held annually in Oxnard. Strawberries are the big treats and are used in strawberry shortcake, strawberry tarts, strawberries dipped in chocolate, strawberry smoothies and strawberry pizza.

Badger Pass Bean Soup

1 (15 ounce) can refried beans
1 (14 ounce) can chicken broth
2 (4 ounce) cans chopped green chilies
2 cloves garlic, minced
2 - 3 jalapeno chilies, seeded, chopped
1 teaspoon chili powder
6 slices bacon
5 ribs celery, chopped
1 bunch green onions with tops, chopped, divided
1 (8 ounce) package shredded cheddar cheese

- Heat refried beans and chicken broth in large saucepan and whisk beans and broth together. Add green chilies, garlic, jalapenos, ¼ teaspoon pepper and chili powder and stir well. Reduce heat to low and stir occasionally.

- Fry bacon in skillet until crisp; drain on paper towels. Saute celery and most of the onions in pan drippings until they are translucent.

- Crumble bacon and add to bean soup. Add onions and celery and pan drippings and stir well. Bring to a boil, reduce heat to low and serve immediately.

- Garnish with remaining onions and cheese. Serves 4.

Two of the ten most populous cities in the U.S., Los Angeles and San Diego, are located in California.

Director's Choice Broccoli-Cheese Soup

This really is an incredible soup!

1 (10 ounce) package frozen chopped broccoli
3 tablespoons butter
¼ onion, finely chopped
¼ cup flour
1 (16 ounce) carton half-and-half cream
1 (14 ounce) can chicken broth
⅛ teaspoon cayenne pepper
½ teaspoon summer savory
1 (8 ounce) package cubed mild Mexican Velveeta® cheese

- Punch several holes in broccoli package and microwave for 5 minutes. Turn package in microwave and cook for additional 4 minutes. Leave in microwave for 3 minutes.

- Melt butter in large saucepan over low heat and saute onion but do not brown.

- Add flour, stir and gradually add half-and-half cream, chicken broth, ½ teaspoon salt, ¼ teaspoon pepper, cayenne pepper and savory. Stir constantly and heat until mixture is slightly thick. Do NOT let mixture come to a boil.

- Add cheese, stir and heat until cheese melts. Add cooked, drained broccoli. Serve piping hot. Serves 4 to 6.

California is known as the Golden State, *the* Land of Milk and Honey, *the* Grape State *and the* El Dorado State. *The official state nickname is the* Golden State.

Redwood Green Chile-Corn Chowder

¼ pound bacon
1 medium onion, minced
1 (15 ounce) can whole kernel corn with liquid
1 (15 ounce) can Mexican diced, stewed tomatoes
2 – 3 fresh Anaheim green chilies, roasted, peeled, seeded,
  chopped
2 large baking potatoes, peeled, cubed
1 teaspoon sugar
1 teaspoon paprika
¼ teaspoon white pepper
1 (5 ounce) can evaporated milk

- Cut bacon into very small pieces and fry until crisp in skillet. Add onion and cook until translucent. Transfer to soup pot.

- Boil 3 cups water and add corn, tomatoes, green chilies, potatoes, sugar, ½ teaspoon salt, paprika and white pepper.

- Cook on medium-low until potatoes are tender. Remove from heat and slowly stir in evaporated milk. Serve immediately. Serves 4 to 6.

Both the giant Sequoia and the coast redwood are recognized as the official state trees of California. The giant Sequoia is protected in Sequoia National Park and the coast redwood which can exceed 300 feet in height grows in a narrow region along California's coast.

Roasted Garlic Soup

4 – 6 cloves garlic, peeled
1 tablespoon olive oil, divided
1 onion, finely chopped
2 (14 ounce) cans chicken broth
4 russet potatoes, peeled, diced
2 teaspoons fresh lemon thyme or ½ teaspoon dried thyme
½ cup low-fat yogurt
½ cup shredded gruyere or jarlsberg cheese
Chives or flat-leaf parsley, chopped
Preheat oven to 375°.

- Remove papery skin from garlic and rub with 1 teaspoon olive oil. Wrap in foil and place in baking dish.

- Bake for 35 to 40 minutes or until soft; let cool. Squeeze garlic from outer skin into bowl and set aside.

- Heat remaining oil in large saucepan over medium heat and saute onion until tender. Add garlic and saute 1 minute.

- Add broth, potatoes and thyme. Cover and simmer until potatoes are very tender, about 25 minutes.

- Puree with yogurt in batches in blender. Serve warm in bowls and top with cheese and chopped chives or parsley. Serves 4.

Vallejo Tomato-Tortilla Soup

8 corn tortillas, cut into strips
Hot canola oil
1 onion, chopped
½ cup finely chopped green bell pepper
½ teaspoon ground cumin
2 teaspoons minced garlic
2 tablespoons canola oil
2 (15 ounce) cans diced tomatoes
1 (4 ounce) can chopped green chilies
3 (14 ounce) cans chicken broth
½ bunch fresh cilantro, very finely chopped
2 cups chopped, cooked chicken breasts
1 (8 ounce) package shredded cheddar cheese

- Fry tortilla strips in hot oil in skillet and drain on paper towels.

- Saute onion, bell pepper, cumin and garlic in 2 tablespoons oil in large soup pot.

- Add diced tomatoes, green chilies, chicken broth, cilantro and chicken and stir occasionally. Cook for 20 to 25 minutes.

- When ready to serve, place a few tortilla strips and some shredded cheese in each bowl, pour soup into bowls and serve immediately. Serves 8.

California's agricultural industry totals about $32 billion annually and generates more than $100 billion in related economic activity

Green Chile Stew Pot (Caldillo)

Caldillo or stew is a traditional dish served on special occasions.

2 pounds round steak, cubed
1 tablespoon seasoned salt
Canola oil
2 onions, chopped
2 potatoes, peeled, diced
2 cloves garlic, minced
6 – 8 fresh Anaheim green chilies, roasted, peeled, seeded, diced

- Sprinkle round steak with seasoned salt, heat oil in large skillet and brown meat over high heat. Put onions, potatoes and garlic in same skillet and cook until onions are translucent.

- Pour all ingredients from skillet into large stew pot. Add chilies, 1 teaspoon salt and ½ teaspoon pepper and enough water to cover.

- Bring to a boil, lower heat and simmer for 1 to 2 hours or until meat and potatoes are tender. Serves 4 to 6.

Arrowhead 15-Minute Turkey Soup

1 (14 ounce) can chicken broth
3 (15 ounce) cans navy beans, rinsed, drained
1 (28 ounce) can diced tomatoes with liquid
2 – 3 cups small chunks cooked white turkey meat
2 teaspoons minced garlic
¼ teaspoon cayenne pepper
Freshly grated parmesan cheese

- Mix all ingredients except cheese in saucepan and heat. Garnish with parmesan cheese before serving. Serves 6.

Half Moon Bay Lobster Chowder

1 small onion, diced
2 tablespoons butter, divided
2 large potatoes, peeled, diced
1½ pounds cooked, chopped lobster or fish
1 (10 ounce) can cream of mushroom soup
½ cup milk

- Cook onions with 1 tablespoon butter in large saucepan over low heat until onions are translucent.

- Add potatoes, remaining 1 tablespoon butter and just enough water to almost cover potatoes. Cover and cook over low heat until potatoes are just tender, about 10 to 15 minutes.

- Add lobster, soup and milk. Cover and cook over low heat for about 20 minutes. (Do not boil.) Season with a little salt and white pepper. Serves 4.

Authentic cioppino originated with the Italian and Portuguese fishermen who emigrated to the San Francisco Bay area. These fishermen and their families used the old cooking traditions and methods and mixed them with the abundance of quality seafood in the northern coastal areas. It resembles the Italian "Zuppa di Pesca" or Seafood Soup.

Morro Bay Fish Chowder

3 tablespoons butter
2 medium onions, diced
1 (1 pint) carton fresh, shucked oysters with liquor
3 large potatoes, peeled, diced
2 cups milk
1 cup half-and-half cream
1½ pounds boneless, skinless fish fillets, cubed
1 bay leaf
Hot sauce
Oyster crackers

- Melt butter in large saucepan and saute onions until they are translucent. Pour oysters with liquor and ¾ cup water into saucepan and mix.

- Add potatoes, cover and cook over low heat until potatoes are slightly tender, about 10 to 15 minutes. (Do not cook too fast.)

- Pour in milk, half-and-half cream, fish, bay leaf and a dash of hot sauce. Cover and cook over low heat for about 20 minutes. Season with salt and pepper. Serve hot with oyster crackers. Serves 4.

Morro Rock in Morro Bay is a sanctuary for the locally endangered peregrine falcon. No public access is permitted.

Angeles Grilled Grapefruit Cups

3 pink or ruby red grapefruit
2 white grapefruit
4 oranges
2 limes
½ cup sherry
¼ cup plus 1 tablespoon packed light brown sugar
3 tablespoons butter

- Cut grapefruit in half, remove interior flesh over large bowl and divide fruit into sections. Save juices in bowl with fruit and set grapefruit shells aside.

- Cut top and bottom from oranges and limes over same bowl and discard them. Cut between pulp and inside peel and remove fruit. Remove any white portions on outside of fruit. Divide into sections and mix with grapefruit in bowl. Discard peels.

- Drain juices from fruit bowl and set aside. Pour sherry over fruit, cover and marinate for 1 hour in refrigerator.

- Place mixed fruit in grapefruit shells and sprinkle brown sugar over fruit. Divide butter equally among fruit in grapefruit shells. Place in 9 x 13-inch baking dish and broil in oven until butter melts and sugar crystallizes.

- Pour remaining juices over top and serve immediately. Serves 6.

Mendocino Melon Boats

2 cantaloupes, chilled
Lettuce leaves
4 cups red and green seedless grapes, chilled
1 cup mayonnaise
⅓ cup frozen orange juice concentrate

- Cut each melon in 6 lengthwise sections and remove seeds and peel. Place lettuce leaves on individual serving plates and arrange melon on top.

- Heap grapes over and around cantaloupe slices.

- Combine mayonnaise and juice concentrate in bowl and mix well. Ladle over fruit. Serves 6.

Salinas Avocado-Artichoke Salad

2 (15 ounce) cans French cut green beans, drained
8 green onions with tops, chopped
¾ cup Italian salad dressing
2 avocados
1 (8 ounce) can artichoke hearts, drained

- Place green beans and onions in serving dish. Pour dressing over mixture and refrigerate for several hours or overnight.

- When ready to serve, chop avocados and artichoke hearts and stir in with beans and onions. Serves 8.

The Artichoke Capital of the world is Castroville, California. In 1947, Norma Jeane Mortenson was crowned the Artichoke Capital's first queen. Norma Jeane later changed her name to Marilyn Monroe.

Pistachio Dessert Salad

1 (20 ounce) can crushed pineapple with juice
1 (3 ounce) package instant pistachio pudding mix
2 cups miniature marshmallows
1 cup chopped pecans
1 (8 ounce) carton whipped topping, thawed

- Place pineapple in large bowl and sprinkle with dry pudding mix.

- Add marshmallows and pecans and fold in whipped topping. Pour into crystal serving dish and refrigerate. Serves 8 to 10.

Golden State Avocado-Spinach Salad

2 ripe avocados
1 (5 ounce) package baby spinach
½ carton grape tomatoes, halved
1 (4 ounce) package crumbled feta cheese
1 small red onion, chopped
⅓ cup coarsely chopped pistachios
Crushed peppercorns

- Just before serving, peel, slice and cube avocados. Mix with remaining ingredients in bowl except dressing. Serve your favorite dressing on the side. Serves 4.

California is the second largest producer of pistachios in the world with a yield of more than 400 million pounds grown annually on 150,000 acres.

Palm Springs Avocado-Grapefruit Salad

4 oranges
4 large, sweet grapefruit
2 tablespoons raspberry vinegar
2 tablespoons honey
Lettuce leaves
2 large avocados

- Grate about 1 tablespoon orange rind. (Do not get any white pith.)

- Peel, break into sections and seed grapefruit and oranges. Mix raspberry vinegar and honey in bowl.

- Pour honey mixture over grapefruit and orange sections and mix. Place fruit sections on bed of lettuce.

- Peel and slice avocados. Place slices on top of fruit and top with grated orange peel. Serve immediately. Serves 4 to 6.

In the late 1850's, the richest gold mine in the world, as well as the deepest mine in North America, was the Kennedy Mine located in Jackson, California.

Simple Avocado Halves

6 ripe avocados
Lemon
Lettuce
1 tablespoon olive oil
1 tablespoon balsamic vinegar
½ - 1 cup shredded Mexican 4-cheese blend

- Peel avocados, remove seeds and cut in half lengthwise. Sprinkle each half with a little lemon juice. Place each avocado half on bed of lettuce.

- In separate bowl, mix oil and vinegar and pour a little into each avocado cavity. Lightly sprinkle a little salt and place shredded cheese on top to serve. Serves 6 to 12.

Los Altos Broccoli-Noodle Salad

1 cup slivered almonds, toasted
1 cup sunflower seeds, toasted
2 (3 ounce) packages chicken-flavored ramen noodles
1 (16 ounce) package broccoli slaw
1 (8 ounce) bottle Italian salad dressing

- Preheat oven to 255°.

- Spread almonds and sunflower seeds on baking sheet and toast for about 10 minutes.

- Break up ramen noodles and mix with slaw, almonds and sunflower seeds in bowl.

- Toss with Italian salad dressing and refrigerate. Serves 12 to 16.

Kickin' Jicama Salad

1 (1 pound) jicama, peeled
1 cup thinly sliced red onion
1 small cucumber with peel, sliced
5 tomatillos, husks removed, washed, sliced
Balsamic vinaigrette dressing
⅛ teaspoon hot sauce

- Slice jicama in ⅛-inch slices and cut each slice into ⅛-inch strips. Place in large container with lid; add red onion, cucumber and tomatillos and toss lightly to mix.

- Pour small amount of dressing and hot sauce over salad, toss to determine correct amount of dressing. Add more dressing if needed, toss and refrigerate for 1 to 2 hours.

- Toss again before serving. Use slotted spoon to remove salad from container and serve in lettuce-lined salad bowl. Serves 4.

Mediterranean Potato Salad

2 pounds new (red) potatoes, quartered
¾ – 1 cup Caesar dressing
½ cup grated parmesan cheese
¼ cup chopped fresh parsley
½ cup chopped roasted red peppers

- Cook potatoes in saucepan in boiling water until fork-tender and drain.

- Pour dressing over potatoes in large bowl.

- Add cheese, parsley and red peppers and toss lightly. Serve warm or chilled. Serves 6 to 8.

Terrific Tortellini Salad

2 (14 ounce) packages frozen cheese tortellini
1 green bell pepper, seeded, diced
1 red bell pepper, seeded, diced
1 cucumber, chopped, drained
1 (14 ounce) can artichoke hearts, halved, rinsed, drained
1 (8 ounce) bottle creamy Caesar salad dressing

- Prepare tortellini according to package directions and drain.

- Combine tortellini, bell peppers, cucumber, artichoke hearts and dressing in large bowl.

- Cover and refrigerate for at least 2 hours before serving. Serves 8 to 10.

Nutty Green Salad

6 cups torn, mixed salad greens
1 medium zucchini, sliced
1 (8 ounce) can sliced water chestnuts, drained
½ cup peanuts
⅓ cup Italian salad dressing

- Toss greens, zucchini, water chestnuts and peanuts in bowl.

- When ready to serve, add salad dressing and toss. Serves 6.

California produces more than 70% of the nation's head lettuce.

California Cobb Salad

½ head lettuce, shredded or torn
½ head romaine, shredded or torn
1 boneless, skinless chicken breast half, cooked, sliced
6 strips bacon, cooked crisp, crumbled
2 eggs, hard-boiled, chopped
2 large tomatoes, chopped, drained
¾ cup plus 2 tablespoons crumbled roquefort cheese, divided
1 large avocado
3 green onions with tops, chopped

- Mix lettuce and romaine in large salad bowl. Arrange chicken on top of greens in one area.

- Repeat for bacon, eggs, tomatoes and ¾ cup roquefort cheese, placing each in separate area.

- Peel and slice avocado and arrange slices in the center.

- Sprinkle remaining roquefort and green onions over top. Serve with Cobb Salad Dressing or your favorite salad dressing.

Cobb Salad Dressing:

¾ cup salad oil
¼ cup olive oil
¼ cup red wine vinegar
1 teaspoon freshly squeezed lemon juice
¾ teaspoon Worcestershire sauce
¼ teaspoon dijon-style mustard
1 clove garlic, minced
¼ teaspoon sugar

- Add all ingredients to bowl and mix well. Season with ½ teaspoon salt and ¼ teaspoon pepper and refrigerate.

- Serve with Cobb Salad. Serves 8.

Spinach Salad with California's Spinach Salad Dressing

8 - 10 ounces baby spinach, stemmed, torn
2 cups strawberries, halved
½ cup pecan pieces
¼ cup red wine vinegar
½ teaspoon dry leaf tarragon, crushed
½ teaspoon dijon-style mustard
1 cup olive oil

- Toss spinach, strawberries and pecans in salad bowl and refrigerate.

- Mix vinegar and tarragon in small saucepan, bring to a boil and remove from heat. Pour vinegar-tarragon mixture into bowl and blend in mustard. Slowly add oil and whisk constantly until it blends well.

- Pour dressing over salad, season with a little salt and pepper and toss well. Serves 3 to 4.

The history of the Cobb Salad is best written by the Brown Derby Restaurant itself. "One night in 1937, Bob Cobb, then owner of The Brown Derby, prowled hungrily in his restaurant's kitchen for a snack.

"Opening the huge refrigerator, he pulled out this and that: a head of lettuce, an avocado, some romaine, watercress, tomatoes, some cold breast of chicken, a hard-boiled egg, chives, cheese and some old-fashioned French dressing. He started chopping. Added some crisp bacon swiped from a busy chef.

"The Cobb salad was born. It was so good, Sid Grauman (Grauman's Chinese Theatre), who was with Cobb that midnight, asked the next day for a 'Cobb Salad". It was so good that it was put on the menu.

"Cobb's midnight invention became an overnight sensation with Derby customers, people like movie mogul Jack Warner, who regularly dispatched his chauffeur to pick up a carton of the mouth-watering salad."

San Joaquin Spring Greens Salad

1 (5 ounce) package fresh spring greens salad mix
¾ cup quartered strawberries, drained
⅓ cup pistachios, coarsely chopped
⅓ cup raisins
1 large ripe avocado
Lemon juice
⅓ cup blue cheese crumbles
Raspberry dressing

- Gently toss spring greens, strawberries, pistachios and raisins in bowl gently and refrigerate.

- Just before serving, peel and slice avocado. Sprinkle a little lemon juice over slices. Sprinkle blue cheese crumbles and avocado on top. Serve dressing with salad. Serves 4.

Luscious Papaya-Chicken Salad

1 (10 ounce) package romaine lettuce, torn
2 ripe papayas, peeled, seeded, cubed
1 large red bell pepper, seeded, sliced
¼ cup lime juice
¼ cup honey
2 teaspoons minced garlic
1 teaspoon dijon-style mustard
3 tablespoons extra-virgin olive oil
2 cups cooked, cubed chicken breasts
⅓ cup pecan pieces, toasted

- Combine lettuce, papayas and bell pepper in large salad bowl.

- Whisk lime juice, honey, garlic, mustard and a little salt in small bowl. Slowly add olive oil in thin stream and whisk dressing until it blends well.

- Pour dressing over salad, add chicken and toss. To serve, sprinkle pecans over top of salad. Serves 6 to 8.

Raisin-Rice Chicken Salad

3 cups instant brown rice
¼ cup (½ stick) butter
3 cups cooked, diced chicken breasts
½ cup golden raisins
½ cup chopped red bell pepper

- Cook brown rice according to package directions. Add butter and a little salt and pepper. While rice is still hot, stir in chicken, raisins and bell pepper. Transfer to serving bowl.

Dressing:

2 tablespoons lemon juice
1 tablespoon dijon-style mustard
2 tablespoons honey
1 teaspoon white wine vinegar
¼ cup slivered almonds, toasted

- Combine lemon juice, mustard, honey and wine vinegar in jar and shake until ingredients blend well. Drizzle over rice-chicken mixture and sprinkle with almonds. Serves 6 to 8.

TIP: Toasting brings out the flavors of nuts and seeds. Place nuts or seeds on baking sheet and bake at 225° for 10 minutes. Be careful not to burn them.

Rainbow Salad

4 cups torn mixed salad greens
3 fresh green onions with tops, chopped
2 medium red apples with peels, diced
1 cup fresh raspberries
½ cup poppy seed dressing

- Toss salad greens, green onions and fruit in bowl.

- Drizzle with dressing and toss. Serves 4 to 6.

Pasta-Turkey Salad Supper

1 (12 ounce) package tri-color spiral pasta
1 (4 ounce) can sliced ripe olives, drained
1 cup broccoli florets
1 cup cauliflower florets
2 small yellow squash, sliced
1 cup halved cherry tomatoes
1 (8 ounce) bottle cheddar-parmesan ranch dressing
1½ pounds cooked hickory-smoked cracked-pepper turkey
  breast, cubed

- Cook pasta according to package directions. Drain and rinse in cold water. Combine pasta, olives, broccoli, cauliflower, squash and tomatoes in large salad bowl.

- Toss with dressing. Arrange turkey over salad. Serve immediately. Serves 8 to 10.

Each man, woman and child eats about 80 tomatoes per person annually in the form of fresh, processed, chopped, stewed tomaotes and ketchup, sauces, juices plus hundreds of consumer products that use tomatoes.

Vegetables and
Side Dishes

Official Tree of California:
Giant Sequoia and Coast Redwood

Official Fossil of California:
Sabre-Toothed Cat

Balboa Pasta with Artichokes, Olives and Prosciutto

1 (10 ounce) package rotini or fusilli pasta
1 (10 ounce) jar artichoke hearts with marinade
3 large tomatoes, seeded, chopped, drained
⅓ cup sliced black olives, drained
6 green onions with tops, chopped
½ pound sliced prosciutto, chopped
1 tablespoon mayonnaise

- Prepare pasta according to package directions. Set aside to cool.

- Mix all remaining ingredients with pasta and serve chilled. Serves 4.

Modesto Pasta with Basil

2½ cups small tube pasta
1 small onion, chopped
2 tablespoons olive oil
2½ tablespoons dried basil
1 cup shredded mozzarella cheese

- Cook pasta in saucepan according to package directions, drain and save about ¼ cup liquid.

- Saute onion in oil in skillet. Stir in basil, 1 teaspoon salt and ¼ teaspoon pepper. Cook and stir for 1 minute.

- Add pasta and about ¼ cup liquid to basil mixture.

- Remove from heat and stir in cheese just until it begins to melt. Serve immediately. Serves 4 to 6.

Monterey Mushroom Pasta

1 onion, chopped
1 cup chopped celery
1 green bell pepper, seeded, chopped
1 red bell pepper, seeded, chopped
1 (8 ounce) carton fresh mushrooms, sliced
6 tablespoons (¾ stick) butter
1⅓ cups orzo pasta
1 (14 ounce) can beef broth
1 tablespoon Worcestershire sauce
¾ cup chopped walnuts
Chopped green onions with tops

- Preheat oven to 325°.

- Saute onion, celery, bell pepper and mushrooms in butter in skillet.

- Cook orzo in beef broth and 1 cup water in saucepan for 10 to 11 minutes and drain.

- Combine onion-mushroom mixture, orzo, Worcestershire, walnuts, and ½ teaspoon each of salt and pepper in large bowl and mix well.

- Transfer to sprayed 2-quart baking dish. Cover and bake for 30 minutes.

- When ready to serve, sprinkle chopped green onions over top of casserole. Serves 8.

Napa Penne with Creamy Goat Cheese and Walnuts

1 (16 ounce) package penne pasta
1 bunch green onions with tops, chopped
1 cup walnut pieces
3 – 4 tablespoons olive oil
1 (4 ounce) carton crumbled goat cheese
1 (8 ounce) carton whipping cream
½ cup shredded romano cheese

- Prepare pasta according to package directions and drain.

- Saute green onions and walnuts in hot oil in skillet over medium heat until onions are translucent. Add drained pasta and goat cheese to skillet, simmer until goat cheese melts and stir frequently. (Do not scorch cheese.)

- Pour in whipping cream and romano cheese and heat on low. Stir until cheeses are hot. Serve immediately. Serves 4 to 6.

The Golden Gate Bridge was completed in 1937 as an extension of US Route 101, also known as the Pacific Coast Highway and what was originally called El Camino Real (the royal road) by Spanish settlers.

Confetti Orzo

This is really good. The alfredo sauce gives it a very mild, pleasing flavor.

8 ounces orzo pasta
½ cup (1 stick) butter
3 cups broccoli florets, stemmed
1 bunch green onions with tops, chopped
1 red bell pepper, seeded, chopped
2 cups chopped celery
1 clove garlic, minced
½ teaspoon cumin
2 teaspoons chicken bouillon granules
1 (8 ounce) carton sour cream
1 (16 ounce) jar creamy alfredo sauce

- Preheat oven to 325°.

- Cook orzo according to package directions; it is best to stir orzo several times during cooking time. Drain.

- While orzo cooks, melt butter in skillet and saute broccoli, onions, red bell pepper, celery, garlic and cumin and cook just until tender-crisp.

- Add chicken bouillon to vegetables and mix well.

- Spoon into large bowl and fold in sour cream, alfredo sauce, 1 teaspoon each of salt and pepper and orzo. Spoon into sprayed 9 x 13-inch baking dish.

- Cover and bake for 30 minutes. Serves 8 to 10.

TIP: This can be refrigerated and baked later. Let it come to room temperature before baking.

Easy Brown Rice and Pine Nuts

1 (6 ounce) box instant brown rice
1 (14 ounce) can beef broth
2 ribs celery, sliced
1 small onion, chopped
¼ cup (½ stick) butter
1 teaspoon grated lemon peel
1 tablespoon chopped fresh cilantro leaves
¼ cup toasted pine nuts

- Cook brown rice according to package directions using beef broth with water to total amount of liquid in package directions. Let stand for 5 minutes.

- Saute celery and onion in butter in skillet over medium heat. Fluff rice and add celery, onion, lemon peel, cilantro and pine nuts. Serves 8.

Carmel Garlic Asparagus

3 – 4 cloves garlic, peeled, minced
¼ cup (½ stick) butter
1 bunch fresh asparagus

- Saute garlic with butter in small saucepan over medium heat. Arrange asparagus spears in large saucepan and pour butter mixture over spears.

- Cover and cook over medium heat for about 10 minutes or until tender. Stir occasionally to coat spears with butter mixture. Asparagus should be slightly crunchy. Serve hot. Serves 4.

La Jolla Asparagus Quiche

1 (9 inch) refrigerated piecrust
¼ cup (½ stick) butter
3 tablespoons flour
1½ cups milk
4 eggs, beaten
1 pound fresh asparagus, trimmed, chopped
½ cup shredded Swiss cheese
¼ cup breadcrumbs

- Preheat oven to 350°.

- Place several sheets of heavy-duty foil in piecrust and over edge. Bake for about 5 minutes. Remove from oven, discard foil and bake for additional 5 minutes.

- Melt butter in saucepan and stir in flour and a little salt. Stir to dissolve all lumps. Cook over medium heat and gradually pour in milk. Continue to stir until mixture thickens.

- Add remaining ingredients except breadcrumbs. Pour quiche mixture into piecrust and sprinkle with breadcrumbs.

- Bake for about 30 minutes or until knife inserted in center comes out clean. Cool slightly, slice into wedges and serve warm. Serves 6.

Thyme-Roasted Asparagus

2 bunches fresh asparagus, trimmed
3 tablespoons olive oil
¾ teaspoon dried thyme

- Preheat oven to 350°.

- Place asparagus in baking dish lined with foil.

- Drizzle with oil and thyme and toss to coat. Sprinkle with a little salt and pepper.

- Bake for 15 minutes. Serves 6.

San Gabriel Pine Nut-Broccoli

1 bunch fresh broccoli, trimmed
¼ cup (½ stick) butter
½ cup pine nuts
⅓ cup golden raisins
2 tablespoons lemon juice

- Break broccoli into florets and steam until tender-crisp. Combine butter, pine nuts and raisins in saucepan and saute for about 3 minutes.

- When ready to serve, add lemon juice to nut mixture and pour over broccoli. Serves 4.

Dude and Dudette Carrots

1 (16 ounce) bunch baby carrots
¾ cup orange juice
2 tablespoons butter
2 tablespoons brown sugar
½ teaspoon ground cumin

- Combine carrots, orange juice, butter, brown sugar, cumin and
  ¼ cup water in saucepan. Cook on medium-high for about
  10 minutes or until carrots are tender and liquid cooks out.
  Serves 6.

Greenhorn Creamed Carrots

¼ cup (½ stick) butter
3 tablespoons flour
1½ cups milk
2 (15 ounce) cans sliced carrots

- Melt butter in saucepan and add flour plus ½ teaspoon salt and
  mix well.

- Add milk, cook over medium heat and stir constantly. Cook
  until mixture thickens.

- In smaller saucepan, heat carrots and drain. Add carrots to
  milk mixture and serve hot. Serves 6 to 8.

*California is the second most populous state in the Western
Hemisphere. The state of Sao Paulo, Brazil is the largest.*

Coronado Chile-Cheese Pie

1½ cups crumbled guacamole-flavored tortilla chips, divided
1 (9 inch) piecrust, baked
1 (15 ounce) can chili beans with liquid
1 (7 ounce) can diced green chilies, drained
3 green onions with tops, chopped
1 (4 ounce) can sliced black olives, drained
1 (8 ounce) carton sour cream
1 (4 ounce) can sliced mushrooms, drained
1 (8 ounce) package shredded Mexican 4-cheese blend

- Preheat oven to 325°.

- Spread 1 cup crumbled chips in piecrust. Combine beans, green chilies, onions and olives in bowl and spread evenly over chips.

- Spoon layer of sour cream next and sprinkle mushrooms on top. Sprinkle evenly with cheese.

- Cover and bake for about 15 minutes. Uncover, sprinkle with remaining chips and bake for additional 15 minutes. Serve immediately. Serves 8.

Grilled Whole Anaheim Chilies

Serve these delicious chilies whole or sliced in strips called rajas.

8 - 10 fresh, whole Anaheim green chilies

- Place chilies on lightly sprayed grill over low heat. Turn frequently because chilies blister and char on outside,. Grill for about 2 to 3 minutes.

- Remove from grill and slide peel away from chilies. Serve whole or cut into narrow strips. Remove seeds to lessen the heat. Serves 6 to 8.

Stuffed Poblano Rellenos

1¼ cups chopped walnuts
1 cup goat cheese crumbles
½ cup ricotta cheese
1 teaspoon cayenne pepper
6 large poblano chilies with stems, roasted, peeled, seeded
5 eggs, beaten
¼ cup flour
1¼ cups milk
Canola oil

- Combine walnuts, goat cheese, ricotta cheese and cayenne pepper in bowl and mix well. Carefully open roasted poblano chilies and stuff cheese mixture into poblanos and close chilies.

- Mix eggs, flour, milk, and ½ teaspoon each of salt and pepper in medium bowl. Dip chilies in egg mixture.

- Heat oil in deep fryer to 350°. Place chilies in hot oil and fry until golden brown. Remove from oil and drain. Serve immediately. Serves 6.

TIP: To roast chilies: Place poblano chilies over open flame or broil in oven until outside turns dark brown and blisters on all sides. (Be careful not to burn holes in skin.) Place peppers in plastic bag, seal and allow to sweat for about 15 to 20 minutes so skin will slide off easily. Remove skins and out through length of pepper on one side. Remove seeds, but leave veins and stem intact.

Grilled Corn-on-the-Cob

Corn-on-the-cob grilled in their own husks is a fun novelty and very tasty. Other veggies like mushrooms, bell pepper, long slices of squash or zucchini, and whole tomatoes are delicious cooked right on the grill.

Fresh corn-on-the-cob in husks
Butter

- Shuck each ear of corn by removing outer husks, but save largest husks.

- Remove all silks on corn and spread butter over corn. Season with salt and pepper and wrap corn in inner husks and large outer husks to hold butter. Tie with long pieces of outer husks.

- Place on grill and cook for 15 to 30 minutes, depending on coals and size of corn. Turn once or twice while cooking. Remove from grill and serve hot. Yields 1 per person.

Major international markets for California's agricultural products include the European Union, Canada, Japan and Mexico.

Canyon Eggplant Frittata

This is a delicious way to serve eggplant for a light lunch and it is rich enough to be served as the main course. You could put it together the day before and cook it just before serving.

3 cups peeled, finely chopped eggplant
½ cup chopped green bell pepper
3 tablespoons extra-light olive oil
1 (8 ounce) jar roasted red peppers, drained, chopped
10 eggs
½ cup half-and-half cream
1 teaspoon Italian seasoning
⅓ cup grated parmesan cheese

- Preheat oven to 325°.

- Cook eggplant and bell pepper in oil in skillet for 2 to 3 minutes, just until tender. Stir in roasted red peppers.

- Combine eggs, half-and-half cream, 1 teaspoon salt, Italian seasoning and ¼ teaspoon pepper in bowl and beat just until they blend well.

- Add eggplant-pepper mixture to egg-cream mixture. Pour into sprayed 10-inch deep-dish pie pan.

- Cover and bake for about 15 minutes or until center sets.

- Uncover and sprinkle parmesan cheese over top. Return to oven for about 5 minutes, just until cheese melts slightly.

- Cut into wedges to serve. Serves 6.

CALIFORNIA REPUBLIC

Merced Green Beans and Mushrooms

½ cup (1 stick) butter, divided
1 small onion, chopped
1 (8 ounce) carton fresh shiitake mushrooms, sliced
2 pounds fresh green beans, trimmed
¾ cup chicken broth

• Melt ¼ cup (½ stick) butter in saucepan, saute onion and mushrooms and transfer to small bowl.

• In same saucepan, melt remaining butter and toss with green beans.

• Pour chicken broth over beans and bring to a boil. Reduce heat, cover and simmer until liquid evaporates and green beans are tender-crisp. Stir in mushroom mixture and season with a little salt and pepper. Serves 8.

Tahoe Green Beans with Pine Nuts

1 (16 ounce) package frozen green beans, thawed
¼ cup (½ stick) butter
¾ cup pine nuts
½ teaspoon garlic powder
½ teaspoon celery salt

• Cook beans in ½ cup water in 3-quart saucepan, covered, for 10 to 15 minutes or until beans are tender-crisp and drain.

• Melt butter in skillet over medium heat and add pine nuts. Cook, stirring frequently, until golden. Add pine nuts to green beans and season with garlic powder, ½ teaspoon salt, ½ teaspoon pepper and celery salt. Serves 6.

Sequoia Onion Casserole

This is a great substitute for potatoes or rice.

3 cups cracker crumbs
½ cup (1 stick) butter, melted, divided
4 cups coarsely chopped onions

- Preheat oven to 300°.

- Combine and mix cracker crumbs and ¼ cup (½ stick) butter in bowl. Place mixture in 9 x 13-inch baking dish and pat down. Saute onions in remaining butter and spread over crust.

Sauce:

1 cup milk
2 eggs, slightly beaten
1 teaspoon seasoned salt
1½ cups shredded cheddar cheese

- Combine milk, eggs, seasoned salt, ¼ teaspoon pepper and cheese in saucepan. Cook over low heat until cheese melts.

- Pour mixture over onions and bake for 45 minutes or until knife inserted in center comes out clean. Serves 6.

Onions come in three colors: white, yellow and red. White onions are used in Mexican dishes and have a slightly sweet flavor. Yellow onions have full flavor and are good for cooking. About 87% of crop production is grown in yellow onions. Red onions are sweeter and are perfect for grilling.

Papas con Chile Verde

2 cups thinly sliced potatoes
½ cup chopped, seeded Anaheim green chilies
1 onion, chopped
1 clove garlic, minced
2 tablespoons olive oil

- Brown potatoes, green chilies, onion, garlic and ½ teaspoon salt in hot oil in large skillet until onions are translucent.

- Add 2 cups water and simmer for about 20 to 25 minutes. Add more water, if needed. Serves 4.

Riverfront Roasted New Potatoes

18 – 20 small, new (red) potatoes with peels
½ cup (1 stick) butter, melted
2 (4 ounce) cans diced green chilies
2 tablespoons fresh snipped parsley
½ teaspoon garlic powder
½ teaspoon paprika

- Steam potatoes in large saucepan with small amount of water until tender. (Test with fork.)

- In separate saucepan, combine butter, green chilies, parsley, garlic powder, 1 teaspoon salt and ½ teaspoon pepper. Heat until ingredients mix well.

- Place potatoes in serving dish, spoon butter mixture over potatoes and sprinkle with paprika. Serves 6 to 8.

Mount Whitney is 14,495 feet above sea level and Bad Water in Death Valley is 282 feet below sea level. Both are located in California. These are the highest and lowest points in the 48 contiguous United States.

Backlot Spinach with Pine Nuts

1 (16 ounce) package frozen leaf spinach, thawed
¼ cup (½ stick) butter
2 cloves garlic, finely minced
5 green onions with tops, chopped
½ teaspoon seasoned salt
¼ teaspoon celery salt
½ cup pine nuts

- Cook spinach according to package directions and drain. Melt butter in saucepan and add garlic, green onions, seasoned salt and celery salt. Mix well, pour over spinach and toss.

- Spoon mixture into a sprayed 2-quart baking dish and sprinkle pine nuts over top. Place under broiler and brown nuts slightly. Serve hot. Serves 6.

The design of California's state flag dates back to 1846 when American immigrants to California were revolting against Mexico. William Todd hand-painted the flag which gave the name "Bear Flag Revolt" to the event. The current California state flag is a modification of the original design and was officially adopted by the legislature in 1911.

El Paseo Spinach Enchiladas

2 (10 ounce) packages chopped spinach, thawed, drained well
1 (1 ounce) packet onion soup mix
1 (12 ounce) package shredded cheddar cheese, divided
1 (12 ounce) package shredded Monterey Jack cheese, divided
12 flour tortillas
1 (16 ounce) carton whipping cream

- Preheat oven to 350°.

- Squeeze spinach between paper towels to completely remove excess moisture.

- Combine spinach and onion soup mix in medium bowl. Blend in half cheddar cheese and half Monterey Jack cheese.

- Lay out 12 tortillas, place about 3 heaping tablespoons spinach mixture down middle of tortilla and roll tortillas.

- Place each filled tortilla, seam-side down in sprayed 9 x 13-inch baking dish.

- Pour cream over enchiladas and sprinkle with remaining cheese.

- Cover and bake for 15 minutes. Uncover and bake for additional 15 minutes. Cool slightly, use spatula to get under each whole enchilada and serve. Serves 8 to 12.

The California State Railroad Museum in Sacramento is one of the largest railroad museums in North America.

Celebrity Squash Mix

1 large spaghetti squash
1 large bell pepper, seeded, chopped
1 large tomato, seeded, chopped
4 – 5 green onions with tops, chopped
3 ribs celery, chopped
½ cup olive oil
½ cup vinegar

- Boil spaghetti squash in water in saucepan for 45 minutes. Remove from water, cut in half and cool.

- Combine bell pepper, tomato, green onions and celery in large bowl.

- In separate bowl mix oil, vinegar and a little salt and pepper and stir well. Pour over bell pepper mixture and stir.

- Remove seeds from squash and scoop out flesh with fork. Add to vegetables and stir well. Cover and refrigerate for several hours before serving. Serves 6.

"The tomato is by definition a fruit because technically it is a ripened ovary of a seed plant; but, in 1893 the U.S. Supreme Court overruled Mother Nature declaring that tomatoes were not fruits, but vegetables." —*California Tomato Growers Association*

Eureka Baked Tomatoes

2 (15 ounce) cans diced tomatoes, drained
1½ cups toasted breadcrumbs, divided
¼ cup sugar
½ onion, chopped
¼ cup (½ stick) butter, melted

- Preheat oven to 325°.

- Combine tomatoes, 1 cup breadcrumbs, sugar, onion and butter in bowl.

- Pour into sprayed 2-quart baking dish and cover with remaining breadcrumbs.

- Bake for 25 to 30 minutes or until crumbs are light brown. Serves 6.

"Eureka!" is the state's motto. The Greek word means, "I have found it!" This is the only state motto in Greek.

Santa Rosa Broccoli-Stuffed Tomatoes

4 medium tomatoes
1 (10 ounce) package frozen chopped broccoli
1 (6 ounce) roll garlic cheese, softened
½ teaspoon garlic salt

- Preheat oven to 375°.

- Cut tops off tomatoes and scoop out flesh. Cook broccoli in saucepan according to package directions and drain well.

- Combine broccoli, cheese and garlic salt in saucepan and heat just until cheese melts. Stuff broccoli mixture into tomatoes and place on baking sheet.

- Bake for about 10 minutes. Serves 4.

Rush Hour Tomatoes

Dijon-style mustard
3 medium tomatoes, halved
¼ cup (½ stick) butter, melted
⅓ cup grated parmesan cheese
⅓ cup seasoned Italian breadcrumbs

- Spread a little dijon-style mustard over cut half of tomatoes. Mix butter, parmesan cheese, breadcrumbs and a little salt and pepper in bowl.

- Divide mixture over mustard-covered tomato halves and pat down. Broil for a few minutes or until breadcrumbs brown. Serves 4.

Baja Grilled Vegetables

Lots of vegetables can be grilled and everyone loves the real flavors an open fire brings out.

Grape tomatoes
Roma tomatoes
Button mushrooms
Bell pepper, green, yellow and red, seeded, quartered
Zucchini, sliced lengthwise
Yellow squash, sliced lengthwise
Sweet onions, peeled, quartered
Jalapenos, seeded, veined
Portobello mushrooms
Asparagus
Eggplant
Poblano peppers
Olive oil

- Lightly coat vegetables with olive oil and a little salt and pepper. Skewer and alternate small vegetables like tomatoes and button mushrooms and place larger vegetables directly on grill.

- (Skewers with onion slice, green bell pepper, grape tomato, button mushroom, yellow bell pepper, another onion slice, etc. make a beautiful vegetable medley.)

- Place on medium-low heat and cook for several minutes until tender.

Vegetable crops in California include artichokes, asparagus, snap beans, broccoli, Brussels sprouts, cabbage, carrots, cauliflower, celery, corn, cucumbers, eggplant, escarole, endive, garlic, greens (collard, kale, mustard), lettuce (head, leaf, romaine), melons (cantaloupe, honeydew, watermelon), mushrooms, onions, bell peppers, chili peppers, pumpkins, radishes, spinach, squash and tomatoes.

Main Dishes

Beef
Chicken
Pork
Seafood

Official Flag of California:

Chico Green Chile-Stuffed Tenderloin

2 cloves garlic, minced
1 medium onion, chopped
1 tablespoon virgin olive oil
1 (4 ounce) can diced green chilies
½ cup shredded Mexican 4-cheese blend
½ cup seasoned breadcrumbs
4 (6 ounce/2 inch) thick beef tenderloin fillets

- Cook garlic and onion in oil in large skillet until they are translucent. Add green chilies, cheese and breadcrumbs. Stir several times and remove from heat.

- Make horizontal slice three-quarters through beef tenderloin fillets. Place green chilies mixture in between the cuts in each fillet and use toothpick to hold mixture in place.

- Grill over charcoal or pan fry in large skillet until done. Serves 4.

There are 19 major professional sports league franchises in the state, more than any other state in the U.S.

Seasoned Beef Tenderloin

3 tablespoons dijon-style mustard
2 tablespoons prepared horseradish
1 (3 pound) center-cut beef tenderloin
½ cup seasoned breadcrumbs

- Combine mustard and horseradish in bowl and spread over beef tenderloin.

- Press breadcrumbs into horseradish-mustard mixture and wrap in foil. Refrigerate for at least 12 hours.

- When ready to bake, preheat oven to 375°.

- Remove wrap and place on sprayed baking pan. Bake for 30 minutes or, for medium rare, heat to 145° on meat thermometer. Let tenderloin stand for 15 minutes before slicing. Serves 6.

Grilled Steak with Garlic-Mustard Sauce

⅓ cup apple juice
2 tablespoons dijon-style mustard
1 tablespoon minced garlic
4 (1 inch) thick boneless beef top strip steaks

- Combine apple juice, mustard, garlic and 1 teaspoon pepper in bowl and mix well. Set aside ¼ cup sauce for basting. Brush steaks with remaining sauce.

- Cook steaks on grill over medium hot coals. Grill for about 15 to 18 minutes or until desired doneness and turn occasionally.

- During last 8 to 10 minutes of grilling, baste steaks with the ¼ cup sauce set aside for basting. Serves 4.

Malibu Dynamite Marinated Beef Kebabs

You will not believe how good this is and how impressive it looks. It is a real treat!

2 – 2½ pounds sirloin steak
Green, red and yellow bell peppers
Large fresh mushrooms
Small onions
Cherry tomatoes

Marinade:

1 cup red wine
2 teaspoons Worcestershire sauce
2 teaspoons garlic powder
1 cup canola oil
¼ cup ketchup
2 teaspoons sugar
2 tablespoons vinegar
1 teaspoon marjoram
1 teaspoon rosemary
½ teaspoon seasoned pepper

- Cut meat into 1½ to 2-inch pieces and quarter bell peppers. Set vegetables aside.

- Mix all marinade ingredients and 1 teaspoon salt in bowl and stir well. Marinate steak 3 to 4 hours.

- Alternate meat, mushrooms, bell peppers, onions and cherry tomatoes on skewers.

- Cook on charcoal grill, turn on all sides and baste frequently with remaining marinade. Discard uncooked marinade. Serves 8.

Six Rivers Spicy Pepper Steak

1½ – 2 pounds sirloin or round steak
2 tablespoons olive oil
1 teaspoon garlic powder
¾ teaspoon ground ginger
1 teaspoon seasoned salt
3 green bell peppers
1 onion, chopped
1 cup sliced celery
2 tablespoons cornstarch
¼ cup soy sauce
1 teaspoon sugar
1 (14 ounce) can beef broth
1 (4 ounce) can sliced mushrooms, drained
1 (10 ounce) can tomatoes and green chilies, drained
Rice or noodles, cooked

- Cut steak into very thin strips. (It will slice easier if frozen for 1 hour.) Heat oil in large skillet or roasting pan, brown steak and add garlic powder, ginger, seasoned salt and ½ teaspoon pepper. Remove meat and saute bell peppers, onion and celery for 3 minutes.

- Dissolve cornstarch in a little cold water in bowl. Add steak to skillet or roasting pan and add soy sauce, sugar, beef broth, cornstarch, mushrooms, and tomatoes and green chilies.

- Bring ingredients to a boil then simmer for 30 minutes. (If you prefer, place in 3-quart baking dish and bake at 350° for 40 minutes.) Serve over rice or noodles. Serves 10 to 12.

Thai Beef, Noodles and Veggies

2 (4.4 ounce) packages Thai sesame noodles
1 pound sirloin steak, cut in strips
Canola oil
1 (16 ounce) package frozen stir-fry vegetables, thawed
½ cup chopped peanuts

- Cook noodles according to package directions. Remove from heat and cover.

- Season sirloin strips with salt and pepper.

- Add half sirloin strips to skillet with a little oil, brown and cook for 2 minutes and remove to bowl. Cook remaining steak and remove to bowl.

- In same skillet, place vegetables and ½ cup water, cover and cook for 5 minutes or until tender-crisp. Remove from heat and add steak strips and toss to mix. Serve over noodles and sprinkle with chopped peanuts   . Serves 6 to 8.

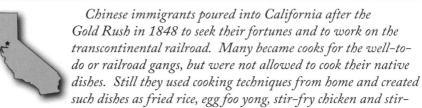

Chinese immigrants poured into California after the Gold Rush in 1848 to seek their fortunes and to work on the transcontinental railroad. Many became cooks for the well-to-do or railroad gangs, but were not allowed to cook their native dishes. Still they used cooking techniques from home and created such dishes as fried rice, egg foo yong, stir-fry chicken and stir-fry vegetables, all of which continue to be served today.

Diablo Pepper Steak

This is an easy way to fix steak!

¼ cup flour
1½ pounds round steak, cut in ½-inch strips
¼ cup canola oil
1 (15 ounce) can diced tomatoes, drained
½ cup chopped onion
1 small clove garlic, minced
1 tablespoon beef bouillon granules
1½ teaspoons Worcestershire sauce
2 large green bell peppers, seeded, cut in strips
Rice, cooked

- Combine flour, ½ teaspoon salt and ¼ teaspoon pepper in bowl and coat steak. Heat oil in large skillet and brown meat on both sides.

- Add tomatoes, 1 cup water, onion, garlic and bouillon. Cover and let simmer for 1 hour 15 minutes or until meat is tender.

- Uncover and add Worcestershire sauce and bell pepper strips. Cover again and simmer for additional 5 minutes. If you like, thicken gravy by mixing 1 tablespoon flour with ¼ cup water. Stir into steak mixture and cook until thickened. Serve over rice. Serves 4 to 6.

Palm Desert Tomato-Cilantro Steak

1 – 1½ pounds well trimmed round steak, tenderized
Flour
Canola oil
2 onions, chopped
5 carrots, sliced
¾ teaspoon garlic powder
1 (15 ounce) can diced tomatoes with liquid
¾ cup salsa
2 teaspoons beef bouillon granules
¼ cup snipped cilantro

- Preheat oven to 325°.

- Cut meat into serving-size pieces and sprinkle with a little salt and pepper. Dredge steak pieces in flour and coat well. Heat oil in large skillet and brown meat on both sides.

- Remove steak to 9 x 13-inch baking dish. Add onions and carrots and cover.

- In same skillet, combine garlic powder, tomatoes, salsa, ½ cup water, beef bouillon, cilantro and 1 teaspoon salt.

- Heat, stir just to boiling point and pour over steak, onions and carrots. Cover and bake for about 1 hour 10 minutes. Serves 6 to 8.

California is the largest producer of processed tomatoes in the world, producing almost half of the world's total production.

Processed tomatoes appear in more foods than most people realize. Here's just a sampling: barbecue sauce, spaghetti sauce, pizza sauce, cocktail sauce, steak sauce, ketchup, hot sauce, chili, diced tomatoes, stewed tomatoes, sun-dried tomatoes, whole peeled tomatoes, tomato sauce, tomato paste, crushed tomatoes, marinades, tomato juice, barbecue chips, Sloppy Joe mix, and pork and beans.

Cabrillo Point Grilled Tri-Tip Roast

1 (2 pound) beef tri-tip roast
1 tablespoon coarsely ground black pepper
3 cloves garlic, minced
4 - 5 large baking potatoes, sliced lengthwise about
    ½-inch thick
Olive oil
½ cup sour cream
¼ cup basil pesto sauce
¼ cup chopped, roasted red peppers

- Season tri-tip with black pepper and garlic and rub into meat. Cook over medium hot grill for about 40 minutes or until meat thermometer reads 140° in the center.

- At same time rub potatoes with olive oil and cook on grill or in the oven until brown on the outside and tender on the inside.

- Wrap tri-tip loosely in foil for several minutes. Mix sour cream and pesto sauce in bowl and dabble over potatoes. Top with roasted peppers. Serves 4 to 6.

Miramar Marinated Tri-Tip Roast

2 cloves garlic, minced
⅔ cup soy sauce
¼ cup canola or virgin olive oil
¼ cup packed light brown sugar
2 tablespoons red wine vinegar
1 teaspoon ground ginger
1 (2 - 3 pound) tri-tip roast

- Mix garlic, soy sauce, oil, brown sugar, vinegar and ginger in bowl. Pour into resealable plastic bag with roast.

- Marinate in refrigerator overnight. Turn plastic bag several times to rotate meat.

- Cook slowly over charcoal fire until meat is tender. Cut thin slices across grain. Serves 6.

Klamath Mountain Savory Rib Roast

1 tablespoon dried thyme
1 tablespoon dried crushed rosemary
1 teaspoon rubbed sage
1 (4 – 5 pound) rib roast

- Preheat oven to 350°.

- Combine thyme, rosemary and sage in small bowl and rub over roast.

- Place roast fat-side up on rack in large roasting pan. Bake for 2 hours to 2 hours 30 minutes or until meat reaches desired doneness.

- Remove roast to warm serving platter and let stand for 10 minutes before slicing. Serves 6 to 8.

Mojave Beef Brisket

1 (4 – 5 pound) trimmed beef brisket
2 tablespoons garlic powder
2 tablespoons seasoned salt
¼ cup liquid smoke
3 tablespoons Worcestershire sauce

- Place brisket inside foil package. Prepare package so marinade will not drip out.

- Season brisket with garlic powder, 2 tablespoons pepper, seasoned salt and pour in liquid smoke and Worcestershire sauce.

- Seal foil tightly, place in baking pan and refrigerate overnight.

- When ready to bake, preheat oven to 300°.

- Place baking pan and brisket in oven and bake for 4 hours or until meat is very tender. Serves 6 to 8.

Gaslight Enchilada Lasagna

1½ pounds lean ground beef
1 onion, chopped
1 teaspoon minced garlic
1 (15 ounce) can enchilada sauce
1 (15 ounce) can stewed tomatoes
1 teaspoon cumin
1 egg, beaten
1½ cups small curd cottage cheese
1 (12 ounce) package shredded 4-cheese blend, divided
8 (8-inch) corn tortillas, torn
1 cup shredded cheddar cheese

- Preheat oven to 325°.

- Cook beef, onion and garlic in large skillet until meat is no longer pink and drain.

- Stir in enchilada sauce, tomatoes, cumin and ½ teaspoon salt. Bring mixture to boil, reduce heat and simmer for 20 minutes.

- Combine egg and cottage cheese in small bowl.

- Spread one-third of meat sauce in sprayed 9 x 13-inch baking dish. Top with half of 4-cheese blend, half tortillas and half cottage cheese mixture. Repeat layers.

- Top with remaining meat sauce and sprinkle cheddar cheese over top.

- Cover and bake for 25 minutes. Uncover and bake for additional 10 minutes. Serves 6 to 8.

Missionary Tamale Loaf

3 eggs, beaten
¾ cup milk
1 cup cornmeal
6 tablespoons (¾ stick) butter, melted
1 large onion, minced
2 teaspoons minced garlic
1½ pounds lean ground beef
1 (15 ounce) can stewed tomatoes
1 (10 ounce) can tomatoes and green chilies
1 (15 ounce) can whole kernel corn, drained
2 tablespoons chili powder

- Preheat oven to 350°.

- Combine eggs, milk, cornmeal and butter in large bowl, stir well and set aside.

- Brown onion, garlic and ground beef in large skillet and drain. Add tomatoes, tomatoes and green chilies, corn, chili powder, and 1 teaspoon salt and cook on medium heat for about 10 minutes.

- Pour into egg-cornmeal mixture and mix well. Pour into sprayed 2 to 3-quart baking dish. Cover and bake for 1 hour. Serves 6 to 8.

Los Angeles has the fourth largest economy compared to all the states in the U.S.

Nothing Fancy Beef Burritos

1 pound ground beef
1 tablespoon chili powder
2 onions, chopped
1 (15 ounce) can refried beans
4 – 6 flour tortillas, warmed
1 (8 ounce) package shredded Mexican 4-cheese blend
1 tomato, chopped
Salsa

- Brown ground beef with 1 teaspoon salt and chili powder in heavy skillet. Drain grease, add onions and cook until onions are translucent.

- Heat refried beans in saucepan. Spread several tablespoons refried beans on warmed flour tortilla.

- Add ground beef, cheese and tomato, roll and fold up 2 ends in package. Serve with salsa. Serves 4 to 6.

Burritos are traditional Mexican sandwiches made with flour tortillas and a filling. Tortillas are rolled one turn, folded over on both ends to enclose the filling and rolled again tightly. Burritos that are deep fried or baked are called chimichangas.

Catalina Island Apricot Chicken

1 cup apricot preserves
1 (8 ounce) bottle Catalina dressing
1 (1 ounce) packet onion soup mix
6 – 8 boneless, skinless chicken breast halves
Rice, cooked

- Preheat oven to 325°.

- Combine apricot preserves, Catalina dressing and soup mix in bowl.

- Place chicken breasts in sprayed 9 x 13-inch baking dish and pour apricot mixture over chicken.

- Bake for 1 hour 20 minutes. Serve with rice. Serves 6 to 8.

TIP: For a change of pace, use Russian dressing instead of Catalina.

Sixty-five percent of California's population can be found in the Greater Los Angeles area, the San Francisco Bay area and the Riverside–San Bernardino area.

Almond-Crusted Chicken

1 egg
¼ cup seasoned breadcrumbs
1 cup sliced almonds
4 boneless, skinless chicken breast halves
1 (5 ounce) package grated parmesan cheese

- Preheat oven to 325°.

- Place egg and 1 teaspoon water in shallow bowl and beat. In separate shallow bowl, combine breadcrumbs and almonds. Dip each chicken breast in egg, then in almond mixture and place in sprayed 9 x 13-inch baking pan.

- Bake for 20 minutes. Remove chicken from oven and sprinkle parmesan cheese over each breast. Bake for additional 15 minutes or until almonds and cheese are golden brown.

Sauce:

1 teaspoon minced garlic
⅓ cup finely chopped onion
2 tablespoons olive oil
1 cup white wine
¼ cup teriyaki sauce

- Saute garlic and onion in oil in saucepan. Add wine and teriyaki sauce and bring to a boil. Reduce heat and simmer for about 10 minutes or until mixture reduces by half.

- When serving, divide sauce among 4 plates and place chicken breasts on top. Serves 4.

San Bernardino Asparagus Chicken

1 (1 ounce) packet hollandaise sauce mix
2 large boneless skinless chicken breasts, cut into strips
Canola oil
1 tablespoon lemon juice
1 (8 ounce) package egg noodles, cooked
1 (15 ounce) can asparagus spears, drained

- Prepare hollandaise sauce according to package directions.

- Cook chicken strips in large skillet with a little oil for
  10 to 12 minutes or until brown and stir occasionally.

- Add hollandaise sauce and lemon juice. Cover and cook for
  additional 10 minutes, stirring occasionally.

- When ready to serve, place chicken over noodles and add hot
  asparagus spears. Serves 6 to 8.

The largest county in the 48 contiguous United States is San Bernardino County near Los Angeles.

The Artichoke Capital of the world is Castroville, California. In 1947, Norma Jeane Mortenson was crowned the Artichoke Capital's first queen. Norma Jeane later changed her name to Marilyn Monroe.

Avalon Artichoke Chicken

6 boneless, skinless chicken breast halves
7 tablespoons butter, divided
1 (14 ounce) jar water-packed artichoke hearts, drained
1 (8 ounce) can sliced water chestnuts, drained
¼ cup flour
1 teaspoon summer savory
1 teaspoon dried thyme
1 (14 ounce) can chicken broth
½ cup whipping cream
1 cup shredded Swiss cheese
1 cup seasoned breadcrumbs

- Preheat oven to 350°.

- Brown chicken breasts in 2 tablespoons butter in skillet. Place chicken breasts in sprayed 9 x 13-inch baking dish.

- Cut each artichoke heart in half and place artichokes and water chestnuts around chicken.

- Melt 3 tablespoons butter in saucepan and stir in flour, ½ teaspoon pepper, summer savory and thyme until smooth.

- Gradually stir in broth and cook on medium-high heat, stirring constantly, until broth thickens. Remove from heat and stir in cream and cheese.

- Blend until cheese melts and pour over chicken, artichokes and water chestnuts.

- Combine breadcrumbs and 2 tablespoons melted butter in bowl and sprinkle over top of casserole. Bake for 35 minutes. Serves 6.

Avalon is the only city on Catalina Island off the coast of southern California. The island is part of Los Angeles County.

China Lake Sweet Pepper Chicken

6 – 8 boneless, skinless chicken breasts halves
2 tablespoons canola oil
⅓ cup cornstarch
⅔ cup sugar
½ cup packed brown sugar
1 teaspoon chicken bouillon granules
1 (15 ounce) can pineapple chunks with juice
1½ cups orange juice
½ cup vinegar
¼ cup ketchup
2 tablespoons soy sauce
¼ teaspoon ground ginger
1 red bell pepper, thinly sliced

- Preheat oven to 325°.

- Brown chicken breasts in large skillet with oil. Place in sprayed 10 x 15-inch baking dish.

- Combine cornstarch, sugar, brown sugar and bouillon granules with several tablespoons water in large saucepan and mix well.

- Drain pineapple and save juice. Add pineapple juice, orange juice, vinegar, ketchup, soy sauce and ginger to cornstarch mixture in saucepan and mix well.

- Cook on high heat, stirring constantly, until mixture thickens. Pour sauce over chicken breasts. Bake for 45 minutes.

- Remove from oven, add pineapple chunks and thinly sliced bell pepper and bake for additional 15 minutes. Serves 6 to 8.

Cilantro-Chicken Breasts

6 boneless, skinless chicken breast halves
3 teaspoons snipped cilantro, divided
1¼ teaspoons ground cumin, divided
2 cups breadcrumbs
Canola oil
3 tablespoons butter
¼ cup flour
2 cups milk
⅓ cup dry white wine
1 (8 ounce) shredded Monterey Jack cheese

- Preheat oven to 350°.

- Pound chicken breast halves to ¼-inch thick with mallet or
  rolling pin. Mix 1 teaspoon each of salt and pepper,
  2 teaspoons cilantro, and 1 teaspoon cumin in bowl. Sprinkle
  seasonings over chicken cutlets and dip in breadcrumbs.

- Heat oil in large skillet and brown chicken on both sides.
  Remove to sprayed 9 x 13-inch baking dish.

- Melt butter in saucepan, blend in flour, ½ teaspoon salt,
  1 teaspoon cilantro and ¼ teaspoon cumin in saucepan. Add
  milk, stir constantly and cook until sauce thickens.

- Remove from heat and stir in wine. Pour sauce over chicken.
  Cover and bake for 45 minutes. Remove from oven, sprinkle
  cheese on top of each piece of chicken and return to oven for
  5 minutes. Serves 6.

*The largest living tree in the world with a trunk
circumference of 102 feet is the General Sherman Tree,
a giant Sequoia located in Sequoia National Park.*

Best Marinated Smoked Chicken

This is smoked chicken at its best!

3 chickens, cut in half
Seasoned pepper
½ cup (1 stick) butter
2 teaspoons Worcestershire sauce
2 dashes hot sauce
2 tablespoons lemon juice
½ teaspoon garlic salt
1 (12 ounce) can lemon-lime carbonated soda

- Sprinkle chicken with seasoned pepper and leave at room temperature for 1 hour.

- Melt butter in saucepan with Worcestershire, hot sauce, lemon juice and garlic salt and add lemon-lime carbonated soda.

- Cook chickens in smoker with charcoal and mesquite-wood fire. Turn often and baste several times with butter-lemon mixture.

- When chicken is done (about 60 minutes) baste once more to keep chicken moist. Serves 8 to 10.

California has the largest economy in the U.S. and was the first to reach one trillion dollars. It is the seventh largest economy compared to all the countries in the world.

Inyo Chicken with Sweet Red Peppers

1 (14 ounce) can chicken broth
1 (8 ounce) can whole kernel corn, drained
2 cups cooked, cubed chicken breasts
1 cup roasted red bell peppers
¼ cup pine nuts, toasted

- Preheat oven to 325°.

- Combine chicken broth, corn, chicken and roasted bell peppers in saucepan over medium-high heat. Cover and simmer for about 10 minutes.

- Spoon into sprayed 7 x 11-inch baking dish, top with pine nuts and bake for 15 minutes. Serves 4.

Orange County Chicken

⅔ cup flour
½ teaspoon dried basil
¼ teaspoon leaf tarragon
2 - 3 tablespoons canola oil
6 boneless, skinless, chicken breast halves
1 (6 ounce) can frozen orange juice concentrate, thawed
½ cup white wine vinegar
⅔ cup packed brown sugar
1 (6 ounce) box long grain-wild rice, cooked

- Preheat oven to 350°.

- Mix flour, 1 teaspoon salt, ½ teaspoon pepper, basil and tarragon in resealable plastic bag. Pour oil into large skillet and heat. Coat chicken in flour mixture and brown both sides of chicken.

- Mix orange juice concentrate, ¼ cup water, vinegar and brown sugar in small bowl. When chicken breasts brown, place in sprayed 9 x 13-inch baking dish, cover with orange juice mixture and bake for 1 hour.

- Serve chicken and orange sauce over rice. Serves 6.

Chimichangas con Pollo

4 - 6 boneless, skinless chicken breast halves, cooked,
   shredded
3 - 4 poblano green chilies, roasted, peeled, chopped
2 tomatoes, peeled, seeded, chopped
1 onion, chopped finely
6 - 8 flour tortillas
1 (8 ounce) package shredded Mexican 4-cheese blend
Canola oil
Red or green chile sauce

- Combine chicken, green chilies, tomatoes and onion in bowl
  and stir well to mix. Divide mixture evenly onto tortillas and
  top with cheese. Fold ends like envelope, roll and secure
  with toothpick.

- Place in deep fryer with oil heated to 350° and fry until golden
  brown. Drain and serve with chile sauce. Serves 6.

Easy Crispy Chicken Tacos

*Everybody goes for this classic. Crispy taco shells with chicken, beef or
fish make great treats.*

8 - 10 taco shells, warmed
4 - 6 boneless, skinless chicken breast halves,
   cooked, chopped
1 cup diced tomato, drained
½ cup diced onion
1 cup chopped lettuce
1 (12 ounce) package shredded cheddar cheese
1 (8 ounce) jar spicy salsa

- Make tacos by filling each taco shell with chicken, tomato,
  onion, lettuce and cheese. Serve with salsa. Serves 6 to 8.

Lime-Salsa Chicken

¼ cup canola oil
1 (10 ounce) jar green chile salsa
1½ tablespoons lime juice
½ teaspoon sugar
1 teaspoon garlic powder
1 teaspoon ground cumin
½ teaspoon oregano
6 boneless, skinless chicken breast halves

- Combine all ingredients except chicken in bowl and mix well. Add chicken breasts and marinate for 3 to 4 hours. Discard marinade.

- Cook over hot coals for about 10 to 15 minutes or until juices run clear. Turn occasionally. Serves 6.

Los Angeles has the fewest number of freeway miles per capita of any American city or urbanized area, which accounts for the congestion on the highways.

Rancho Tomatillo-Chicken Enchiladas

2 (13 ounce) cans tomatillos, drained
1 (7 ounce) can chopped green chilies
2 tablespoons canola oil
1 onion, chopped
1 clove garlic, minced
1 (14 ounce) can chicken broth
¼ cup olive oil
12 corn tortillas
3 cups shredded, cooked chicken
1 (12 ounce) packages shredded Monterey Jack
   cheese, divided
1 (8 ounce) carton sour cream

- Preheat oven to 350°.

- Combine tomatillos and green chilies in blender and process. Heat 2 tablespoons oil in large skillet, add onion and garlic and cook until onion is translucent.

- Stir in tomatillo puree and chicken broth. Simmer until sauce reduces to consistency of canned tomato sauce.

- In separate skillet, heat ¼ cup oil and cook tortillas for about 3 seconds on each side. Dip softened tortilla into tomatillo mixture. Lay sauced tortilla on plate. Place ¼ cup chicken and 2 tablespoons cheese across tortilla and roll to close.

- Place enchilada, seam-side down in 10 x 15-inch baking pan. Repeat until all tortillas are filled. Spoon remaining sauce over enchiladas.

- Cover and bake for about 35 minutes. Top with remaining cheese and bake uncovered for additional 10 minutes. When ready to serve, top each enchilada with 1 tablespoon sour cream. Serves 8 to 12.

Surfin' Chicken Enchiladas

3 cups cooked, shredded chicken
1 (4 ounce) can chopped green chilies
1 (7 ounce) can green chile salsa
1 onion, minced
6 chicken bouillon cubes
1 (1 pint) carton whipping cream
Canola oil
10 corn tortillas
1 (12 ounce) package shredded Monterey Jack cheese
1 (8 ounce) carton sour cream

- Preheat oven to 350°.

- Combine chicken, green chilies, green chile salsa and onion in bowl.

- Combine bouillon cubes, ½ teaspoon salt and cream in saucepan and heat until bouillon dissolves, but do not boil.

- Heat oil in skillet and dip each tortilla into oil for about 5 seconds to soften. Drain on paper towels. Dip each tortilla into saucepan with cream and coat each side. Fill each tortilla with chicken mixture.

- Roll and place seam-side down in sprayed 9 x 13-inch baking dish. Pour remaining cream over enchiladas and sprinkle with cheese. Bake for 30 to 35 minutes. When ready to serve, top with dollops of sour cream. Serves 6 to 10.

Tequila-Lime Chicken

½ cup lime juice
¼ cup tequila
1½ teaspoons chili powder
1½ teaspoons minced garlic
1 teaspoon seeded, diced jalapeno pepper
6 boneless, chicken breast halves with skin

• Combine all ingredients except chicken in large resealable plastic bag. Add chicken breasts, seal bag and turn to coat. Refrigerate for 10 hours or overnight.

• Remove breasts from marinade and sprinkle chicken with a little salt and pepper. Discard marinade.

• Grill skin-side down for 5 to 7 minutes. Turn and grill for 10 minutes or until it cooks thoroughly. Remove to platter, cover and let stand for 5 minutes before serving. Serves 6.

Chicken Oriental

1 (10 ounce) jar sweet-and-sour sauce
1 (1 ounce) packet onion soup mix
1 (16 ounce) can whole cranberry sauce
6 boneless, skinless chicken breast halves

• Preheat oven to 325°.

• Combine sweet-and-sour sauce, onion soup mix and cranberry sauce in bowl.

• Place chicken breasts in sprayed 9 x 13-inch shallow baking dish. Pour cranberry mixture over chicken breasts.

• Cover and bake for 30 minutes. Uncover and bake for additional 25 minutes. Serves 6.

Sunny Stir-Fry Chicken

Canola oil
1 pound chicken tenders, cut into strips
1 (16 ounce) package frozen broccoli, cauliflower and carrots
1 (8 ounce) jar stir-fry sauce
1 (12 ounce) package chow mein noodles

- Heat a little oil in 12-inch wok or skillet and stir-fry chicken strips over high heat for about 4 minutes.

- Add vegetables and stir-fry for additional 4 minutes or until vegetables are tender. Stir in stir-fry sauce and cook just until mixture is hot. Serve over chow mein noodles. Serves 8 to 10.

Sweet-and-Sour Chicken and Veggies

1 (3 ounce) package chicken-flavored ramen noodles
1 (16 ounce) package frozen broccoli, cauliflower and carrots
3 boneless, skinless, cooked chicken breast halves, cut
   in strips
⅔ cup sweet-and-sour sauce
1 tablespoon soy sauce

- Cook noodles and vegetables in 2 cups water (reserve seasoning packet) in large saucepan for 3 minutes or until liquid absorbs.

- Add seasoning packet, chicken, sweet-and-sour sauce and soy sauce. Heat on medium-low heat and stir until all is thoroughly hot. Serves 6.

San Francisco Chop Suey

In the 1890's a Chinese viceroy, Li Hung Chang, asked the chef at the Palace Hotel in San Francisco to prepare vegetables with a little meat "job suey" or cut into small pieces. This was the dish now known as "Chop Suey".

1 cup snow peas
½ pound bok choy
3 ribs celery
1 onion
1 pound chicken, beef or pork
3 tablespoons cornstarch
1 cup soy sauce
¼ cup olive oil
½ cup chopped mushrooms
¼ pound mung bean sprouts, drained
Noodles or rice, cooked

- Cut snow peas, bok choy, celery, onion and meat in 2-inch strips about ¼ inch wide. Mix cornstarch with 3½ cups water in bowl and stir until cornstarch dissolves. Add soy sauce and stir well.

- Heat olive oil in skillet over medium high heat. After oil is hot, carefully add peas, bok choy, celery, onion, meat and mushrooms and cook until meat is barely pink inside. Add bean sprouts and mix well.

- Add soy sauce mixture to skillet and bring to a boil. Cook, stirring constantly, about 3 to 4 minutes or until meat is done. Drain and serve over noodles or rice. Serves 4.

Orange-Glazed Cornish Hens

1 cup fresh orange juice
2 tablespoons plus ½ teaspoon peeled, minced fresh ginger,
   divided
1 tablespoon soy sauce
3 tablespoons honey
2 (1½ pound) cornish hens, halved

- Preheat oven to 400°.

- Combine orange juice, 2 tablespoons minced ginger, soy
  sauce and honey in saucepan and cook on high heat, stirring
  constantly, for 3 minutes or until thick and glossy.

- Place hens in sprayed 9 x 13-inch baking pan and sprinkle
  ½ teaspoon ginger and ½ teaspoon each of salt and pepper
  over birds.

- Spoon glaze mixture over hens and bake for 25 minutes.
  Brush glaze over hens several times while cooking.
  Serves 2.

*California's gross state product is almost two trillion dollars.
Its chief economic industries include agriculture in the Central
Valley, entertainment in Hollywood, technology in the Silicon
Valley, and wine production in the Napa and Sonoma Valleys
as well as the Santa Barbara and Paso Robles areas.*

Southern California Turkey Burgers

2 pounds ground turkey
1 (16 ounce) jar hot chipotle salsa, divided
8 slices Monterey Jack cheese
Sesame seed hamburger buns

- Preheat broiler.

- Combine ground turkey with 1 cup salsa in large bowl. Mix well and shape into 8 patties.

- Place patties on broiler pan and broil for 12 to 15 minutes. Turn once during cooking. Top each patty with cheese slice and heat just long enough to melt cheese.

- Place burgers on buns, spoon heaping tablespoon salsa over cheese and top with remaining half of bun. Serves 6 to 8.

Six Rivers Turkey Tenders

Canola oil
1 pound turkey tenders
Rice, cooked

- Place a little oil in heavy skillet and cook turkey tenders for about 5 minutes on each side or until they brown.

Glaze:

⅔ cup honey
2 teaspoons peeled grated fresh ginger
1 tablespoon marinade for chicken
1 tablespoon soy sauce
1 tablespoon lemon juice

- Combine all glaze ingredients, mix well and pour into skillet with turkey. Bring mixture to a boil, reduce heat and simmer for 15 minutes. Serve over rice. Serves 6.

TIP: *As a time-saver, you might want to try the package of rice that can be microwaved for 90 seconds and it's ready to serve.*

Creamy Turkey Enchiladas

1 onion, finely chopped
3 green onions with tops, chopped
2 tablespoons butter
½ teaspoon garlic powder
1 (7 ounce) can chopped green chilies, drained
2 (8 ounce) packages cream cheese, softened
3 cups cooked, diced turkey
8 (8 inch) flour tortillas
1 (1 pint) carton whipping cream
1 (16 ounce) package shredded Monterey Jack cheese

- Preheat oven to 350°.

- Saute onion and green onions in butter in large skillet.

- Add garlic powder, ½ teaspoon salt and green chilies and stir in cream cheese. Heat on low, stir until cream cheese melts and add turkey.

- Lay out 8 tortillas and spoon about 3 heaping tablespoons turkey mixture on each tortilla. Roll tortillas and place seam-side down in sprayed 9 x 13-inch baking dish.

- Pour whipping cream over enchiladas and bake for 25 minutes. Remove from oven, sprinkle with cheese and bake for additional 10 minutes. Serves 8.

California raises more turkeys than any other state in the U.S.

Hawaiian Aloha Pork

This is great served over rice.

2 (1 pound) lean pork tenderloins
1 tablespoon canola oil
1 (15 ounce) can pineapple chunks with juice
1 (12 ounce) bottle chili sauce
1 teaspoon ground ginger
Rice, cooked

- Cut pork in 1-inch cubes. Season pork tenderloins with salt and pepper and brown on medium-high heat in skillet with oil.

- Add pineapple with juice, chili sauce and ginger.

- Cover and simmer for 30 minutes. Serve over rice. Serves 6 to 8.

Prizing-Winning Pork Tenderloin

⅔ cup soy sauce
⅔ cup olive oil
2 tablespoons crystallized ginger, finely chopped
2 tablespoons fresh lime juice
1 teaspoon garlic powder
2 tablespoons minced onion
2 (1 pound) pork tenderloins

- Combine soy sauce, olive oil, ginger, lime juice, garlic powder and minced onion in bowl and pour over pork tenderloins. Marinate for about 36 hours. Discard marinade.

- Cook over charcoal fire for about 45 minutes. Serves 6 to 8.

Mexican Pork Tenderloin with Zucchini

2 pounds pork tenderloin, cubed
1 small onion, diced
1 green bell pepper, seeded, diced
2 cloves garlic, minced
1 teaspoon ground cumin
3 tomatoes, diced
1½ pounds Mexican squash or zucchini, cubed
1 (15 ounce) can whole kernel corn, drained

- Brown pork in skillet over medium heat and add onion and bell pepper. Cover and cook on low for 15 minutes.

- Add garlic, cumin and tomatoes and cook for additional 10 minutes.

- Add squash, cover and cook for 20 minutes. Add corn and 1 teaspoon salt and simmer for additional 20 minutes. Serves 6 to 8.

The fields of yellow poppies that bloom in the spring and the Gold Rush of 1848 are said to be the reasons for the state legislature to make the Golden State the official state nickname of California in 1968.

Roasted Red Pepper Tenderloin

2 (1 pound) pork tenderloins
1 (.04 ounce) packet ranch dressing mix
2 red bell peppers, roasted, seeded, chopped
2 Anaheim green chilies, roasted, seeded, chopped
2 jalapenos, seeded, chopped
1 (8 ounce) carton sour cream

- Brown tenderloins in large skillet and place in 6-quart oval slow cooker.

- Combine ranch dressing mix, red bell peppers, green chilies, jalapenos and ½ cup water in bowl and spoon over pork tenderloins. Cover and cook on LOW for 4 to 5 hours.

- When ready to serve, remove tenderloins from slow cooker. Stir sour cream into sauce in slow cooker. Serve over tenderloin slices. Serves 6.

The Shasta-Cascade area located in the northeastern corner of California is home to eight national and state parks, six national forests as well as two giant glaciated volcanoes, Mt. Shasta at 14,164 feet and Mt. Lassen at 10,457 feet located in the Trinity Alps and Cascade mountain ranges.

Pork Loin with Apricot Glaze

1 (3½ - 4 pound) center-cut pork loin
1 tablespoon olive oil
Seasoned pepper
1 teaspoon dried rosemary
1 cup dry white wine or cooking wine
1½ cups apricot preserves

- Preheat oven to 350°.

- Rub pork loin with olive oil and sprinkle seasoned pepper and rosemary over roast. Place loin in shallow roasting pan. Pour wine and 1 cup water into pan, cover and roast for 1 hour.

- Remove pan from oven and spoon about 1 cup pan drippings into small bowl. Add apricot preserves and mix well. Pour mixture over pork, reduce oven to 325°, cover and return to oven.

- Continue to roast for additional 1 hour and baste 2 to 3 times with pan drippings.

- Set aside pork for 15 minutes before slicing. Remove roast from drippings, place in glass baking dish and slice.

- Serve immediately or pour drippings into separate container and refrigerate both. When ready to serve, heat drippings and pour over roast. Warm roast at 350° for 20 minutes. Serves 8.

Nine out of every ten tomatoes grown in the U.S. are grown in California. In addition, over 85% of all home gardeners in the U.S. grow tomatoes.

Apple Valley Pork Chops

These pork chops just melt in your mouth!

6 thick-cut pork chops
Flour
Canola oil
3 baking apples

- Preheat oven to 325°.

- Dip pork chops in flour and coat well.

- Brown pork chops in oil in skillet and place in sprayed
  9 x 13-inch baking dish. Add ⅓ cup water to dish. Cover and
  bake for 45 minutes.

- Peel, halve and seed apples and place half apple over each
  pork chop. Return to oven for 5 to 10 minutes. (DO NOT
  overcook apples). Serves 6.

*Agriculture is the largest economic industry in the state and
includes fruit, vegetables, dairy products and wine primarily.*

Tangy Pork Chops

4 - 6 pork chops
¼ cup Worcestershire sauce
¼ cup ketchup
½ cup honey

- Preheat oven to 325°.

- Brown pork chops in skillet. Place in shallow baking dish.
  Combine Worcestershire, ketchup and honey in bowl. Pour
  over pork chops.

- Cover and bake for 20 minutes; uncover and bake for
  additional 15 minutes. Serves 4 to 6.

Pork Chops with Black Bean Salsa

2 teaspoons chili powder
2 tablespoons olive oil
6 thin-cut, boneless pork chops
1 (15 ounce) can black beans, rinsed, drained
1 (24 ounce) refrigerated citrus fruit, drained
1 ripe avocado, sliced
⅔ cup Italian salad dressing

- Combine chili powder and ½ teaspoon salt in bowl. Rub oil
  over pork chops, sprinkle chili powder mixture over chops and
  rub into meat.

- Place pork chops in skillet over medium heat and cook for
  about 5 minutes on both sides.

- For salsa, combine beans, fruit and avocado in bowl and toss
  with salad dressing. Serve with pork chops. Serves 6.

Apple-Glazed Pork Roast

1 (12 ounce) jar apple jelly
4 teaspoons dijon-style mustard
3 teaspoons lemon juice, divided
¼ teaspoon garlic powder
1 (3 - 4 pound) pork loin roast
3 tablespoons brandy

- Preheat oven to 350°.

- Melt jelly in small saucepan over low heat. Stir in mustard and 1 teaspoon lemon juice and set aside. Rub roast with a little pepper and garlic powder.

- Place on rack in foil-lined shallow roasting pan and bake for about 45 minutes. Remove from oven, brush with jelly mixture and bake for additional 20 minutes.

- Brush once more with jelly mixture, reduce heat to 325° and bake for additional 1 hour. Remove roast to warm platter.

- Scrape any browned drippings into remaining jelly mixture. Add 2 teaspoons lemon juice and brandy to mixture, bring to a boil and turn heat off.

- To serve, pour sauce on plate and place thin slices of roast on top or serve roast on platter with sauce. Serve 6 to 8.

Palo Alto Apricot-Baked Ham

1 (12 - 15 pound) whole ham, bone-in, fully cooked
Whole cloves
2 tablespoons dry mustard
1¼ cups apricot jam
1¼ cups packed light brown sugar

- Preheat oven to 450°.

- Trim skin and excess fat from ham. Place ham on rack in large roasting pan.

- Insert whole cloves in ham every inch or so. Be sure to push cloves into ham surface as far as they will go.

- Combine dry mustard and apricot jam in bowl and spread over surface of ham. Pat brown sugar over jam.

- Place in oven and immediately reduce heat to 325° and bake for 15 minutes per pound. (The high heat causes a sugary crust to form on ham which keeps juices inside.)

- When ham is tender, remove from oven, allow ham to stand for 20 minutes and remove from pan to carve. Serves 10 to 12.

Researchers have found that tomatoes have a large amount of lycopene in them. Lycopene has more than twice the amount of powerful antioxidants than vitamins E and C . The high vitamin, mineral and nutrient values of tomatoes may help slow down the aging process and some degenerative diseases such as cancers, cardio-vascular disease and blindness.

Big Sur Fish Tacos

¾ pound boned white fish
2 tablespoons lime juice
Canola oil
6 – 8 corn tortillas
Shredded lettuce
Finely chopped tomatoes

- Season fish with lime juice and pepper. Cook fish in skillet with a little oil for about 2 minutes on each side until fish flakes easily. Shred each piece of fish and set aside.

- Wrap about 5 tortillas in slightly damp paper towel and heat tortillas in microwave for 45 seconds.

- Place about 2 tablespoons shredded fish, lettuce and tomatoes in tortilla and fold over. Serve immediately with pesto.

Pesto:

1 cup packed cilantro leaves
2 teaspoons lime juice
1 teaspoon minced garlic
¼ cup parmesan cheese
⅓ cup olive oil

- Mix all ingredients in bowl and serve with Big Sur Fish Tacos. Serves 6.

Two Years Before the Mast was written by Richard Henry Dana, who was the inspiration for the name of the seaside community of Dana Point.

San Jose Grilled Tuna with Roasted Chile Salsa

4 - 5 poblano chilies
2 mild jalapeno peppers
1 red bell pepper
1 yellow bell pepper
1 large sweet onion, minced
4 - 5 cloves garlic, minced
¼ cup extra-virgin olive oil
¼ cup fresh lime juice
¼ cup snipped cilantro or oregano
4 - 6 tuna steaks

- To roast poblano chilies, hold over open-flame gas burner with long metal fork or broil in oven until outside turns dark brown on all sides. (Be careful not to burn holes through skin.)

- Place chilies in resealable plastic bag, seal and allow to sweat for about 15 to 20 minutes so skin will slide off easily. Remove skins and cut through length of chile on one side. Remove seeds, but leave veins intact.

- Remove seeds and veins from jalapenos and bell peppers. Chop or mince peppers and mix with all remaining ingredients except fish in bowl. Add a little salt and pepper.

- Cook tuna steaks on each side for about 3 minutes over hot coals or until grill marks show. Remove from grill and check center of steaks; tuna is done when steaks are still pink in center. Do not overcook and dry out fish.

- Serve hot with salsa on top. Serves 4 to 6.

In 1925 one of California's giant Sequoia trees was designated as the National Christmas Tree. It is now over 265 feet high and is the third largest tree in the world..

Bayside Red Snapper

1 (8 ounce) can tomato sauce
1 (4 ounce) can chopped green chilies
1 clove garlic, minced
1 pound red snapper fillets

- Mix tomato sauce, green chilies and garlic in small bowl. Place snapper fillets on microwave-safe dish and brush tomato sauce mixture evenly over red snapper.

- Cover with plastic wrap. Microwave on HIGH for about 3 minutes, rotate dish and microwave for 2 minutes.

- Check snapper to see if it flakes easily. If not, microwave for additional 2 minutes and check to see if meat is flaky. Serves 6.

Seafood Enchiladas with Tomatillo Sauce

4 green onions with tops, chopped
1 red bell pepper, seeded, chopped
4 tomatoes, seeded, chopped
1 clove garlic, minced
2 tablespoons canola oil
¾ pound redfish or red snapper, flaked
¾ pound shrimp, peeled, chopped
12 corn tortillas
1 (8 ounce) package shredded Monterey Jack cheese

- Preheat oven to 350°.

- Saute green onions, bell pepper, tomatoes and garlic in oil in skillet until onions are translucent.

- Add fish and shrimp, cook until shrimp turn pink and remove from heat.

- In separate skillet or griddle over low heat, soften corn tortillas.

- Scoop seafood mixture evenly into center of tortilla and sprinkle cheese on top. Roll tortilla tightly and lay seam-side down in sprayed 9 x 13-inch baking dish.

Tomatillo Sauce:

4 green onions with tops, chopped
1 clove garlic, minced
1 tablespoon canola oil
3 jalapeno peppers, stemmed, seeded, chopped
10 tomatillos, peeled
1 (8 ounce) carton sour cream
1 cup chicken broth
¼ cup snipped cilantro leaves

- Saute green onions and garlic in oil in skillet until onions are translucent. Place onions and garlic in blender and add all remaining ingredients. Blend until it reaches smooth consistency and pour over enchiladas.

- Bake for 10 to 15 minutes. Serves 4 to 6.

Grilled Swordfish with Cilantro-Citrus Sauce

3 large pink grapefruit
3 cloves garlic, minced
2 teaspoons chili powder
2 teaspoons ground cumin
½ cup canola oil
¼ cup white wine
4 – 5 (1 inch) swordfish steaks
2 teaspoons butter
Cornstarch
¼ cup snipped cilantro

- Squeeze 1 grapefruit to measure ¾ to 1 cup juice in 4-cup measuring cup. Peel remaining grapefruit, split into sections and refrigerate until ready to use.

- Add garlic, chili powder, cumin, 1 teaspoon salt, oil and white wine to grapefruit juice and mix.

- Place swordfish steaks in flat, glass baking dish and pour marinade over steaks. Cover dish and refrigerate for about 1 hour.

- Prepare charcoal or wood fire and grate. Before grilling, pour about ½ cup marinade from swordfish dish into small saucepan and add butter. Pour remaining liquid into measuring cup.

- Add cornstarch to liquid in measuring cup and stir until it dissolves. Pour liquid with cornstarch into saucepan with butter mixture and bring to a boil. Reduce heat and cook until sauce thickens slightly.

- Add cilantro and simmer while steaks cook. Place steaks on grill for about 3 to 5 minutes and turn to cook other side. Cook for about 3 minutes or just until fish is not quite translucent in center.

- To serve, put each swordfish steak on plate and pour several tablespoons cilantro sauce over top of each. Garnish with grapefruit sections and serve immediately. Serves 4 to 5.

Grilled Swordfish Steaks with Avocado Salsa

4 green onions with tops, finely diced
8 - 10 grape tomatoes, quartered
2 whole pickled jalapenos, seeded, chopped
¼ cup fresh lime juice
¼ cup snipped fresh cilantro
Cracked black pepper
4 (1 inch) thick swordfish steaks
3 ripe avocados

- Mix green onions, tomatoes, jalapenos, lime juice, cilantro, ¾ teaspoon salt and a little cracked black pepper in medium bowl and refrigerate.

- Grill swordfish steaks on each side for about 3 minutes or until grill marks show. Check center of steaks and remove from grill when steaks are almost white. Do not overcook; fish will dry out when overcooked.

- Peel avocados, chop and stir into salsa. Serve swordfish steak and top with avocado salsa. Serves 4.

The annual Avocado Festival is held in Fallbrook which claims the title of Avocado Capital of the World. More avocados are grown in California than in any other state.

Lemon-Dill Halibut

½ cup mayonnaise
2 tablespoons lemon juice
½ teaspoon grated lemon peel
1 teaspoon dill weed
1 pound halibut fillets

- Combine mayonnaise, lemon juice, lemon peel and dill weed in bowl until they blend well.

- Place fish on sprayed grill or broiler rack. Brush with half sauce. Grill or broil for 3 to 5 minutes, turn and brush with remaining sauce.

- Continue grilling or broiling for 3 to 5 minutes or until fish flakes easily with fork. Serves 4 to 6.

Camp Rainbow Trout

2 (1 pound) fresh, whole rainbow trout
Flour
Butter
1 lemon

- Clean trout and remove head and gills, but leave skin intact. Make several diagonal slices on both sides of fish.

- Pour flour into flat pan, add a little salt and pepper and stir. Dredge each fish in flour until both sides are coated with flour.

- Melt just enough butter to cover bottom of heavy skillet and add fish. Cook until fish is moist, but flaky on the inside and golden brown on the outside. Serve with lemon slices. Serves 2 to 4.

Rainbow Trout Skillet

2 (1 pound) rainbow trout fillets
½ cup (1 stick) plus 3 tablespoons butter, divided
10 – 12 large cloves garlic, minced
3 small green onions with tops, minced
3 tablespoons white wine
1 egg
1 – 3 tablespoons canola oil
1 lemon, sliced

- Wash and pat dry trout fillets.

- Melt ½ cup butter in skillet and saute garlic and onions over medium heat until they are translucent. Add white wine and simmer while fish cooks.

- Beat egg slightly with 1 tablespoon water in bowl and dip each fillet into egg mixture. In separate skillet, heat oil and 1 tablespoon butter and place fillets to cook over medium heat.

- Turn once, add 1 to 2 tablespoons butter (if needed) and remove when fish flakes in thickest part.

- Arrange fish on platter, keep warm and pour warm garlic sauce over fish just before serving. Garnish with lemon slices. Serves 2.

Morro Bay is a working fishing community northwest of San Luis Obispo on Highway 1. In the 1940's, it developed an abalone fishing industry until the supply was depleted from overfishing. Fisherman still fish commercially for halibut, rockfish, albacore and sole. Oysters are farmed artificially in the back bay.

Six Rivers Grilled Steelhead

1 whole cleaned steelhead
Onion, minced
Celery, diced
Parsley, snipped
Fresh garlic cloves, minced
Butter
Bacon

- Use these basic ingredients with any size steelhead. Fill cavity of fish with onion, celery, parsley, garlic and butter and season with a little salt and pepper.

- Wrap entire fish with bacon slices. Wrap several times in heavy-duty foil to prevent any leakage. Cook over hot charcoal fire for about 10 minutes on each side. The larger the fish, the longer it will need to cook. Serves 2.

California produces 99% of the nation's agricultural crops for almonds, artichokes, clingstone peaches, dried plums, figs, olives, persimmons, pomegranates, raisins, ladino clover seed, sweet rice and walnuts.

Craggy Shores
Pistachio-Buttered Salmon

½ cup (1 stick) butter
8 - 10 leaves fresh basil, minced
1 clove garlic, minced
Lime juice
¼ cup shelled pistachios
4 (6 ounce) thick, skinless salmon fillets
½ cup white wine

- Preheat oven to 350°.

- Blend butter, basil, garlic, a little lime juice and pistachios in food processor until smooth and set aside or refrigerate until ready to use.

- Rinse and dry salmon fillets and place in sprayed, glass baking dish. Pour white wine over fillets and season with a little salt and pepper.

- Bake until slightly opaque, about 5 minutes. (Do not overcook.) Remove from oven and spread butter mixture over top. Continue baking until fillets are still slightly pink inside. Serves 4.

California is the second largest producer of pistachios in the world with a yield of more than 400 million pounds grown annually on 150,000 acres.

Baked Salmon with Fresh Herbs

¾ cup mayonnaise
¾ cup freshly grated parmesan cheese
1 bunch green onions, chopped
1 tablespoon chopped fresh parsley
1 tablespoon chopped fresh basil
1 tablespoon freshly chopped thyme
3 tablespoons minced red bell pepper
Juice of ½ lemon
Scant ⅛ teaspoon cayenne pepper
1½ pounds salmon fillets with skin

- Preheat oven to 350°.

- Combine mayonnaise, parmesan, green onions, parsley, basil, thyme, bell pepper, lemon juice, ½ teaspoon salt, ¼ teaspoon pepper and cayenne pepper in medium bowl.

- Place salmon, skin-side down on sprayed shallow baking dish. Spread mayonnaise-herb mixture over salmon to within ½ inch of edges. Bake for 20 to 25 minutes or just until flaky. Do not overcook. Serves 4 to 6.

Simple Salmon Bake

Olive oil
4 (6 ounce) salmon fillets
½ cup shelled, minced pistachios
¼ cup minced fresh cilantro
Black peppercorns, crushed

- Preheat oven to 350°.

- Spread olive oil lightly on both sides of salmon fillets.

- Mix pistachios, cilantro and black peppercorns in shallow bowl. Dredge both sides of fillets in pistachio mixture and pat down.

- Place fillets in sprayed baking dish and bake for about 10 to 15 minutes or until fillets are opaque, but still moist. Serves 4.

Carmel Crab Pasta

½ cup (1 stick) butter
½ onion, finely chopped
1 bell pepper, seeded, chopped
1 teaspoon dried summer savory
1 teaspoon dried parsley flakes
1 teaspoon dried basil
½ teaspoon celery salt
1 teaspoon lemon pepper
2 (15 ounce) cans diced tomatoes
1 (15 ounce) can Italian stewed tomatoes
½ cup dry white wine
1 pound cooked crabmeat or lobster
1 pound angel hair pasta, cooked
Freshly grated parmesan cheese

- Melt butter in large saucepan and saute onion and bell pepper. Stir in summer savory, parsley, basil, celery salt, lemon pepper, ½ teaspoon salt and tomatoes and bring to a boil.

- Add wine and simmer for 5 minutes. Add crabmeat and simmer for 2 minutes.

- Place warm pasta in serving dish and top with crab mixture. Serve with parmesan cheese. Serves 6 to 8.

In 2005, California cultivated more than 500,000 acres of wine grapes.

- *Over 300,000 tons of grapes are grown annually.*

- *Over 17 million gallons of wine are produced annually.*

- *California accounts for 90% of the wine production in the U.S.*

Morro Bay Stuffed Crab

¼ bell pepper, seeded, finely diced
1 small onion, finely diced
2 ribs celery, finely diced
¼ cup (½ stick) butter
8 ounces lump crabmeat
1 tablespoon marinade for chicken
1 tablespoon ketchup
1 (8 ounce) carton whipping cream
1 cup seasoned breadcrumbs
Crab shells

- Preheat oven to 350°.

- Saute bell pepper, onion and celery in butter in saucepan and set aside.

- Combine remaining ingredients (except shells) in bowl and add onion-celery mixture.

- Spoon into crab shells and bake for 30 to 35 minutes. Serves 2 to 4.

The suggested serving of whole cooked crab is 2 pounds per person which equals 1 pound after it is cleaned and cracked.

California Rolls

4 nori sheets
1 tablespoon wasabi powder
2 seedless cucumbers
2 avocados
2 Alaska king crab legs, thawed
Lemon juice
3 cups cooked sushi rice
¼ cup sesame seeds, toasted
Soy sauce
Wasabi
Ginger

- Hold nori sheets over high heat with tongs and dry roast until pieces turn green. Place 1 sheet on sudare or bamboo mat.

- Mix wasabi powder with 1 tablespoon water in bowl to make paste. Peel cucumbers, avocados and crab and slice into thin strips. Sprinkle a little lemon juice over avocados.

- Spread ¾ cup sushi rice over nori sheet and leave 1 inch bare at far side making small ledge of rice. Spread about 1 teaspoon wasabi paste down center of rice.

- Sprinkle one-fourth of sesame seeds evenly over rice. Lay one-fourth of crab meat on side closest to you. Lay one-fourth of cucumber and one-fourth avocado firmly next to it.

- Roll mat over once away from you, but leave 1 inch nori sheet sticking out. Press ingredients together to make roll firm and tight. Press mat to tighten roll. Remove mat, again press roll to make it tight and form circle or square.

- Cut into bite-size pieces and serve with soy sauce, wasabi and ginger. Yields 4 rolls and about 32 pieces.

Top-Shelf Tequila Shrimp

1½ pounds medium shrimp, shelled, veined
¼ cup (½ stick) butter
2 tablespoons canola oil
2 cloves garlic, minced
3 tablespoons tequila
1½ tablespoons lime juice
½ teaspoon chili powder
¼ cup coarsely chopped fresh cilantro
Rice, cooked
Lime wedges

- Rinse and pat shrimp dry with paper towels. Heat butter and oil in large skillet over medium heat. Add garlic and shrimp and cook for about 2 minutes, stirring occasionally.

- Stir in tequila, lime juice, ½ teaspoon salt and chili powder. Cook for additional 2 minutes or until most liquid evaporates and shrimp are pink and glazed.

- Add cilantro, serve over rice and garnish with lime wedges. Serves 6.

Fisherman's Beer Shrimp

2 (12 ounce) cans beer
3 tablespoons pickling spice
Lemon slices
2 pounds fresh shrimp

- Pour beer in stew pot and turn on high heat.

- Add pickling spice, lemon slices and ½ teaspoon salt. When mixture steams, add shrimp and stir well. Make sure there is enough liquid to cover or almost cover shrimp.

- Cook just until shrimp turn pink, remove from pot and drain. Serves 4 to 6.

TIP: For larger amounts, use 1½ to 2 tablespoons pickling spice per pound and enough beer to cover shrimp.

Golden State Pasta and Shrimp

2 tablespoons butter
1 tablespoon olive oil
½ pound fresh peeled, veined shrimp
½ poblano pepper, seeded, slivered
½ red bell pepper, seeded, sliced
¼ red onion, thinly sliced
1 clove garlic, minced
2 tablespoons snipped cilantro leaves
2 tablespoons tequila or gin
½ teaspoon seasoned salt
¼ teaspoon chili powder
½ teaspoon cumin
⅓ cup half-and-half cream
2 cups cooked angel-hair pasta
Grated parmesan cheese

- Heat butter and oil in large skillet. Add shrimp and cook for about 8 minutes. When shrimp are pink and firm, drain and set aside.

- Add peppers, onion, garlic and cilantro to skillet and saute until just barely tender. Remove vegetables and set aside.

- Add tequila to skillet and swirl it around pan. Add seasoned salt, chili powder, cumin and half-and-half cream. Allow sauce to thicken slightly.

- Return shrimp and vegetables to skillet and toss until mixture heats and coats shrimp with cream. Serve immediately over pasta. Garnish with parmesan cheese. Serves 6.

Oceanside Grilled Lemon Shrimp

½ cup (1 stick) butter
2 tablespoons Worcestershire sauce
½ teaspoon minced garlic
½ teaspoon celery salt
2 tablespoons lemon juice
2 – 2½ pounds shelled shrimp, drained

- Melt butter in saucepan and add Worcestershire sauce, garlic, celery salt and lemon juice.

- Place shrimp in bowl and pour butter mixture over shrimp. Marinate at room temperature for about 2 hours.

- Grill shrimp for about 3 to 5 minutes (according to size) and baste with butter mixture. Shrimp will turn pink when done. Serves 4 to 5.

Pan-Seared Shrimp Ancho

3 – 4 ancho chilies
½ cup extra-virgin olive oil
6 – 8 cloves garlic, minced
2 pounds fresh shrimp, shelled, veined
Cracked black pepper
Rice, cooked

- Clean ancho chilies well with dry cloth, heat for several minutes in lightly oiled skillet and soak in hot water for about 30 minutes.

- Dry chilies, remove stems and seeds and slice in long, thin strips. Place in large cast-iron or heavy skillet with garlic and about ¼ to ½ cup hot oil. Cook for about 1 to 2 minutes.

- Add shrimp and cook until they turn pink. Season with a little salt and cracked black pepper and serve over rice or with bread and salad. Serves 8.

Seaport Shrimp Cayenne

½ cup (1 stick) butter
2 pounds shrimp, shelled, veined
½ cup green onions with tops, chopped
½ cup chopped celery
½ cup dry white wine
½ teaspoon cayenne pepper
1 tablespoon crab boil seasoning
½ cup taco sauce
1 tablespoon lemon juice

- Melt butter in skillet and saute shrimp, green onions and celery until shrimp are pink and onion is translucent.

- Add wine, cayenne pepper, crab boil, taco sauce, lemon juice, and ½ teaspoon each of salt and pepper and stir well. Cover and simmer for about 5 minutes before serving. Serves 8.

Sunny Shrimp Toss

2 pounds medium shrimp, cooked, peeled, veined
2 large tomatoes, seeded, diced
2 bunches green onions with tops, minced
2 (4 ounce) cans diced green chilies, drained
½ cup minced cilantro
1 - 1½ cups Italian salad dressing
4 teaspoons honey
¼ teaspoon hot pepper sauce
Lettuce leaves

- Mix shrimp, tomatoes, green onions, green chilies and cilantro in bowl.

- In separate bowl, mix salad dressing, honey and hot pepper sauce and pour over shrimp mixture. Cover and refrigerate for 1 to 2 hours before serving. Stir mixture several times.

- Serve each portion on lettuce leaf. Serves 4 to 6.

Whiskeytown's Steamed Lobster

1 onion, quartered
3 ribs celery, quartered
¼ cup pickling spice
1½ cups (3 sticks) butter, melted
2 (1 pound) live lobsters

- Cover vegetables, pickling spice and 1 teaspoon salt with at least 2 to 3 inches water in large soup pot. Bring to a rolling boil. Place lobster in steamer basket, add to pot and cover tightly.

- Steam for about 10 to 15 minutes. Add water, if needed. Check for doneness with small claw. Serve with melted butter. Serves 4.

TIP: *If you want to kill lobsters before putting them into a steamer, make a large cut from 1½ inches behind eyes to between eyes and through head.*

Grilled California Spiny Lobster

4 (1 pound) live California spiny lobsters
⅓ cup olive oil
¼ cup red wine vinegar
3 cloves garlic, crushed
⅓ cup minced green onions with tops
1 cup (2 sticks) butter, melted
2 lemons, halved

- Fill large soup pot with enough water to cover lobsters.

- Cook lobsters in boiling water for 4 minutes and remove. When cool enough to handle, remove head and claws. Slice tail in half lengthwise on the underneath side and open shell about halfway.

- Mix oil, vinegar, garlic and green onions in bowl and brush onto lobster. Grill over hot coals for about 3 to 4 minutes on each side. Baste lobster with remaining oil-vinegar mixture. Serve hot with melted butter and lemon halves. Serves 4.

Sweets

Cakes
Pies
Cookies
Desserts

Official Song of California:
"I Love You, California"

Official Dance of California:
West Coast Swing

Official Folk Dance of California:
Square Dance

Diablo Red Devil Cake

2 cups sugar
2 cups flour
½ cup shortening
½ cup (1 stick) butter
¼ cup cocoa
½ cup buttermilk*
2 eggs, beaten
1 teaspoon baking soda
1 teaspoon vanilla

- Preheat oven to 350°.

- Combine sugar and flour in bowl. Combine shortening, butter, 1 cup water and cocoa in saucepan; bring to a boil. Pour over flour mixture while still hot.

- Add buttermilk, eggs, baking soda and vanilla and beat well. Pour mixture into sprayed, floured 10 x 15-inch baking pan.

- Bake for 20 to 25 minutes. Cake is done when toothpick inserted in center comes out clean.

Frosting:

½ cup (1 stick) butter
¼ cup cocoa
6 tablespoons milk
1 (1 pound) box powdered sugar
1 teaspoon vanilla
1 cup chopped pecans
Several dashes red food coloring

- While cake is baking, prepare frosting. Combine butter, cocoa and milk in saucepan and bring to a boil; remove from heat. Add powdered sugar and vanilla and mix well. Add pecans and red food coloring.

- Spread on cake while both are still hot. Serves 20 to 24.

*TIP: To make buttermilk, mix 1 cup milk with 1 tablespoon lemon juice or vinegar and let milk stand for about 10 minutes.

Chocolate Pudding Cake

1 (18 ounce) box milk chocolate cake mix
1¼ cups milk
⅓ cup canola oil
3 eggs

- Preheat oven to 350°.

- Combine all ingredients in bowl and beat well. Pour into sprayed 9 x 13-inch baking pan.

- Bake for 35 minutes or until toothpick inserted in center comes out clean.

Frosting:

1 (14 ounce) can sweetened condensed milk
¾ (16 ounce) can chocolate syrup
1 (8 ounce) carton whipped topping, thawed
⅓ cup chopped pecans

- Combine sweetened condensed milk and chocolate syrup in small bowl and mix well.

- Pour mixture over cake and let soak. Refrigerate for several hours.

- Spread whipped topping over cake and sprinkle with pecans. Refrigerate.

Countryside Poppy Seed Cake

3 cups sugar
1¼ cups shortening
6 eggs
3 cups flour
¼ teaspoon baking soda
1 cup buttermilk*
3 tablespoons poppy seeds
2 teaspoons almond extract
2 teaspoons vanilla
2 teaspoons butter flavoring

- Preheat oven to 325°.

- Cream sugar and shortening in large bowl until mixture is light and fluffy. Add eggs, one at a time, and blend well.

- In separate bowl, sift flour, baking soda and ½ teaspoon salt. Alternately add dry ingredients and buttermilk to sugar mixture a little at a time.

- Add poppy seeds and flavorings and blend well. Pour into sprayed, floured bundt pan. Cook for 1 hour 15 minutes or when toothpick inserted in center comes out clean. Cool.

Glaze:

1½ cups powdered sugar
⅓ cup lemon juice
1 teaspoon vanilla
1 teaspoon almond extract

- Combine all ingredients in bowl and mix well. Pour over top of cool cake and let some glaze run down sides of cake. Serves 18.

TIP: To make buttermilk, mix 1 cup milk with 1 tablespoon lemon juice or vinegar and let milk stand for about 10 minutes.

Kahanamoku Kahlua Cake

3 eggs, separated
1¼ cups sugar, divided
½ cup (1 stick) butter, softened
1 cup packed light brown sugar
2¼ cups flour
½ cup cocoa
1½ teaspoons baking soda
⅔ cup strong cold brewed coffee
⅔ cup Kahlua® liqueur

- Preheat oven to 350°.

- Beat egg whites in bowl until frothy, pour in ¾ cup sugar and beat until stiff peaks form. Set aside.

- In separate bowl, cream butter, brown sugar and ½ cup sugar until fluffy. Beat in egg yolks one at a time.

- Sift flour, cocoa and baking soda in bowl. Add to creamed mixture alternately with coffee and Kahlua® liqueur and blend well. Fold egg whites into batter.

- Pour into sprayed, floured bundt pan and bake for 55 to 60 minutes. Cake is done when toothpick inserted in center comes out clean.

- Cool for about 10 to 15 minutes before removing cake from pan. Cool completely before frosting.

Frosting:

1 cup powdered sugar
2 tablespoons cocoa
2 - 3 tablespoons Kahlua® liqueur

- Blend powdered sugar, cocoa and Kahlua® liqueur in bowl, drizzle over top and let some drip down sides of cake. Serves 18.

Sweet Angel Cake

1½ cups powdered sugar
⅓ cup milk
1 (8 ounce) package cream cheese, softened
1 (3.5 ounce) can flaked coconut
1 cup chopped pecans
1 (12 ounce) carton whipped topping, thawed
1 large bakery angel food cake, torn into bite-size pieces
1 (20 ounce) can cherry pie filling

- Beat powdered sugar, milk and cream cheese in bowl. Fold in coconut and pecans, stir in whipped topping and cake pieces. Spread in large 9 x 13-inch glass dish and refrigerate for several hours.

- Add pie filling by tablespoons on top of cake mixture. (It will not cover cake mixture, but it will just be in clumps, making a pretty red and white dessert.) Refrigerate. Serves 18 to 20.

California grows more than 75% of all the strawberries in the U.S.

Fresno is known as the Raisin Capital of the World.

Apple Valley's Best Fresh Apple Cake

1½ cups canola oil
2 cups sugar
3 eggs
2½ cups sifted flour
½ teaspoon baking soda
2 teaspoons baking powder
½ teaspoon ground cinnamon
1 teaspoon vanilla
3 cups peeled, grated apples
1 cup chopped pecans

- Preheat oven to 350°.

- Mix oil, sugar and eggs in bowl and beat well.

- In separate bowl, combine flour, ½ teaspoon salt, baking soda, baking powder and cinnamon. Gradually add flour mixture to sugar mixture.

- Add vanilla, fold in apples and pecans and pour into sprayed, floured tube pan.

- Bake for 1 hour. While cake is still warm, invert onto serving plate.

Glaze:

2 tablespoons butter, melted
2 tablespoons milk
1 cup powdered sugar
1 teaspoon vanilla
¼ teaspoon lemon extract

- Mix all ingredients in bowl and drizzle over cake while cake is still warm. Serves 18 to 20.

Redondo Cherry-Pineapple Cake

1 (20 ounce) can crushed pineapple, drained
1 (20 ounce) can cherry pie filling
1 (18 ounce) box yellow cake mix
1 cup (2 sticks) butter, softened
1¼ cups chopped pecans

- Preheat oven to 350°.

- Place all ingredients in bowl and mix with spoon.

- Pour into sprayed, floured 9 x 13-inch baking dish. Bake for 1 hour 10 minutes. Serves 18 to 20.

Quick Apple Cake

1 (18 ounce) box spiced cake mix
1 (20 ounce) can apple pie filling
2 eggs
½ cup chopped walnuts

- Preheat oven to 350°.

- Combine all ingredients in bowl and mix very thoroughly with spoon until all lumps from cake mix are gone. Pour into sprayed, floured bundt pan.

- Bake for 50 minutes. Cake is done when toothpick inserted in center comes out clean. Serves 18.

TIP: You may substitute any other pie filling when making this cake.

Orange Cove's Orange-Date Cake

4 cups flour
1 teaspoon baking soda
1 cup (2 sticks) butter, softened
2½ cups sugar
4 eggs
1½ cups buttermilk*
1 teaspoon orange extract
1 tablespoon grated orange peel
1 (11 ounce) can mandarin oranges
1 (8 ounce) package chopped dates
1 cup chopped pecans

- Preheat oven to 350°.

- Sift flour and baking soda in bowl and set aside. In separate bowl, cream butter and sugar, add eggs one at a time and beat well. Add buttermilk and dry ingredients alternately and end with dry ingredients.

- Add orange extract and peel and beat well. Stir in oranges, dates and pecans.

- Pour into sprayed bundt pan and bake for 1 hour 15 minutes or toothpick inserted in center comes out clean. Remove from oven and pour glaze over cake while still in pan.

Glaze:

½ cup orange juice
1¼ cups sugar
1 teaspoon grated orange peel
½ teaspoon orange extract

- Mix orange juice, sugar, orange peel and extract in saucepan. Bring to a boil and cool. Pour glaze slowly over cake. Serves 18.

*TIP: *To make buttermilk, mix 1 cup milk with 1 tablespoon lemon juice or vinegar and let milk stand for about 10 minutes.*

Newport Pistachio-Lime Pie

2 cups vanilla wafer crumbs
¾ cup chopped pistachio nuts or pecans, divided
¼ cup (½ stick) butter, softened
1 (8 ounce) package cream cheese, softened
1 (14 ounce) can sweetened condensed milk
¼ cup lime juice
1 (3 ounce) package instant pistachio pudding mix
1 (8 ounce) can crushed pineapple with juice
1 (8 ounce) carton whipped topping, thawed

- Preheat oven to 350°.

- Combine crumbs, ¼ cup nuts and butter in bowl and press firmly into 9-inch springform pan. Bake for 8 to 10 minutes and cool.

- Beat cream cheese in large bowl until fluffy, gradually beat in sweetened condensed milk, lime juice and pudding mix and beat until smooth.

- Stir in ½ cup nuts and pineapple and fold in whipped topping.

- Pour into springform pan and refrigerate overnight. Serves 8.

The top 10 commodities in California include milk and cream, grapes, nursery products, almonds, cattle, lettuce, hay, strawberries, floriculture and tomatoes.

California Dream Pie

1 (8 ounce) package cream cheese, softened
1 (14 ounce) can sweetened condensed milk
1 (5 ounce) package vanilla instant pudding mix
1 (8 ounce) carton whipped topping, thawed
2 (6 ounce) ready graham cracker piecrusts
1 (20 ounce) can strawberry pie filling

- Beat cream cheese and sweetened condensed milk in bowl until smooth. Add pudding mix and ½ cup water, mix and refrigerate for 15 minutes. Fold in whipped topping, pour into 2 piecrusts and freeze.

- When ready to serve, remove from freezer and place in refrigerator for 45 minutes before slicing and serving. Spoon about ¼ cup pie filling on each slice of pie. (You could use other pie filling flavors, if you like.) Serves 12.

TIP: Use 2 chocolate ready piecrusts. Pour 2 or 3 tablespoons chocolate ice cream topping over pie and top with chocolate shavings.

More than $100 million of strawberries are grown on acres around Oxnard. Strawberries are shipped across the U.S. and to Germany and Japan.

Creamy Lemon Pie

1 (8 ounce) package cream cheese, softened
1 (14 ounce) can sweetened condensed milk
¼ cup lemon juice
1 (20 ounce) can lemon pie filling
1 (6 ounce) ready graham cracker piecrust

- Beat cream cheese in bowl until smooth and creamy. Add sweetened condensed milk and lemon juice and beat until mixture is creamy.

- Fold in lemon pie filling and stir well. Pour into piecrust and refrigerate for several hours before slicing and serving. Serves 6 to 8.

Strawberry-Cream Cheese Pie

2 (10 ounce) packages frozen, sweetened strawberries, thawed
2 (8 ounce) packages cream cheese, softened
⅔ cup powdered sugar
1 (8 ounce) carton whipped topping, thawed
1 (6 ounce) ready chocolate piecrust
Fresh Strawberries

- Drain strawberries and set aside ¼ cup juice.

- Combine cream cheese, juice, strawberries and powdered sugar in bowl and beat well.

- Fold in whipped topping and spoon into piecrust. Refrigerate overnight and garnish with fresh strawberries. Serves 8.

The Central Valley of California from Sacramento to Bakersfield is, acre for acre, the richest agricultural area in the world.

Capistrano Lime-Margarita Pie

1 (14 ounce) can sweetened condensed milk
2 eggs, separated
½ cup sugar
⅓ cup fresh lime juice
1½ ounces tequila
1 ounce triple sec liqueur
1 (6 ounce) ready graham cracker piecrust
¼ cup sugar
½ cup whipping cream, whipped
Lime slices

- Preheat oven to 350°.

- Combine sweetened condensed milk, egg yolks, sugar, lime juice, tequila and triple sec liqueur in medium bowl and mix well.

- In separate bowl, beat egg whites until slightly stiff and fold them into egg yolk-sugar mixture. Spoon mixture into graham cracker crust. Bake for 25 minutes or until set. Let pie cool.

- Fold sugar into whipped cream in bowl and spread over cooled pie. Refrigerate pie for several hours before serving. Garnish each piece of pie with thin lime slice. Serves 6 to 8.

Corona Strawberry-Margarita Pie

¼ cup frozen pink lemonade concentrate, thawed
2 tablespoons tequila
2 tablespoons triple sec liqueur
1 teaspoon grated lime peel
1 pint fresh strawberries, sliced
1 quart strawberry ice cream, softened
1 (6 ounce) ready graham cracker piecrust, chilled
Strawberries

- Mix lemonade, tequila, triple sec liqueur, lime peel and strawberries in large bowl. Fold in softened ice cream. Work quickly so ice cream will not melt completely.

- Spoon mixture into chilled crust and freeze. Take out of freezer for about 10 minutes before slicing to serve. Garnish with strawberries. Serves 6 to 8.

Easy Chocolate Pie

1 (8 ounce) milk chocolate candy bar
1 (16 ounce) carton whipped topping, thawed, divided
¾ cup chopped pecans
1 (9 inch) baked piecrust

- Break candy into small pieces in saucepan and melt over low heat. Remove and cool for several minutes.

- Fold in two-thirds whipped topping, mix well and stir in pecans.

- Pour into piecrust and spread remaining whipped topping over top and refrigerate for at least 8 hours. Serves 8.

Lemon Grove Tropical Cheesecake

1¼ cups graham cracker crumbs
½ cup flaked coconut
½ cup chopped pecans
2 tablespoons light brown sugar
¼ cup (½ stick) butter, melted
2 (8 ounce) packages cream cheese, softened
1 (14 ounce) can sweetened condensed milk
3 eggs
¼ cup frozen orange juice concentrate, thawed
1 teaspoon pineapple extract
1 (20 ounce) can pineapple pie filling, divided
1 cup sour cream

- Preheat oven to 300°.

- Combine graham cracker crumbs, coconut, pecans, brown sugar and butter in bowl. Press firmly into 9-inch springform pan and set aside.

- Beat cream cheese in large bowl until fluffy. Gradually beat in sweetened condensed milk.

- Add eggs, juice concentrate and pineapple extract and mix well. Stir in ¾ cup pineapple pie filling.

- Pour into sprayed springform pan. Bake for 1 hour or until center is set.

- Spread top with sour cream and bake for additional 5 minutes. Cool, spread remaining pineapple pie filling over cheesecake and refrigerate. Serves 10 to 12.

White Chocolate Cheesecake

2 cups graham cracker crumbs
1 cup slivered almonds, finely chopped
¼ cup (½ stick) butter, softened
8 ounces white chocolate
4 (8 ounce) packages cream cheese, softened
¾ cup sugar
5 eggs
2 tablespoons flour
1 teaspoon vanilla
Strawberries or raspberries
Sugar

- Preheat oven to 275°.

- Combine graham cracker crumbs, almonds and butter in bowl and mix well. Press into 10-inch springform pan. Melt white chocolate in double boiler, stir until smooth and remove from heat.

- Beat cream cheese in bowl until smooth and fluffy and add sugar. Beat in eggs, one at a time, and add flour and vanilla. Mix until smooth and fold in melted white chocolate.

- Pour mixture over graham cracker crust and bake for 60 minutes or until top is firm. Cool completely, cover and refrigerate overnight. Slice strawberries (leave raspberries whole), sprinkle on a little sugar and refrigerate overnight.

- To serve, remove sides of springform pan and slice. Spoon ¼ cup fruit over each slice of cheesecake. Serves 10 to 12.

TIP: The best way to slice cheesecake is to use a sharp knife, clean after each slice, then dip knife in water before slicing the next piece.

Valley Date-Pecan Tarts

1 (8 ounce) package pitted, chopped dates
1½ cups milk
½ cup flour
1½ cups sugar
3 eggs, beaten
1 teaspoon vanilla
1 cup chopped pecans
8 tart shells, baked, cooled
1 (8 ounce) carton whipping cream
3 tablespoons powdered sugar

- Combine dates, milk, flour and sugar in heavy saucepan and cook for about 3 minutes, stirring constantly.

- Stir in eggs and ¼ teaspoon salt and continue cooking, stirring constantly, for additional 5 minutes. Stir in vanilla and pecans. Pour into baked tart shells and cool.

- Whip cream in bowl and add powdered sugar. Top each tart with whipped cream and refrigerate. Serves 8.

California produces about 99.5% of all the dates in the U.S. Indio is known as the Date Capital of the World.

Almond-Fudge Shortbread

1 cup (2 sticks) butter, softened
1 cup powdered sugar
1¼ cups flour
1 (12 ounce) package chocolate chips
1 (14 ounce) can sweetened condensed milk
½ teaspoon almond extract
1 (2.5 ounce) package chopped almonds, toasted

- Preheat oven to 350°.

- Beat butter, powdered sugar and ¼ teaspoon salt in bowl and stir in flour. Pat into sprayed 9 x 13-inch baking pan and bake for 15 minutes.

- Melt chocolate chips with sweetened condensed milk in medium saucepan over low heat and stir until chips melt. Stir in almond extract.

- Spread evenly over shortbread and sprinkle with almonds. Refrigerate for several hours or until firm and cut into bars. They may be stored at room temperature.
  Yields 2 dozen cookies.

California produced more than 12 billion dollars worth of chocolate and cocoa products. California produced more than 7 billion dollars worth of non-chocolate confectionary products.

Chinese Cookies

1 (6 ounce) package chocolate chips
1 (6 ounce) package butterscotch chips
1 cup salted peanuts
1 (3 ounce) can chow mein noodles

- Melt chocolate and butterscotch chips in large saucepan. Add peanuts and noodles and mix well.

- Drop by teaspoonfuls onto wax paper. Refrigerate just to harden. Yields 2 dozen cookies.

Seven-Layer Cookies

½ cup (1 stick) butter
1 cup crushed graham crackers
1 (6 ounce) package semi-sweet chocolate bits
1 (6 ounce) package butterscotch bits
1 (3.5 ounce) can flaked coconut
1 (14 ounce) can sweetened condensed milk
1 cup chopped pecans

- Preheat oven to 350°.

- Melt butter in 9 x 13-inch baking pan. Sprinkle remaining ingredients in order listed.

- Do not stir or mix and bake for 30 minutes. Allow to cool before cutting. Yields 2 dozen cookies.

Sierra Nuggets

1 cup (2 sticks) butter, softened
1 cup packed brown sugar
1½ cups sugar
1 tablespoon milk
2 teaspoons vanilla
2 eggs
1 cup crushed corn flakes
3 cups quick-cooking oats
1½ cups flour
1 teaspoon baking soda
2 teaspoons ground cinnamon
¼ teaspoon ground nutmeg
⅛ teaspoon ground cloves
½ cup flaked coconut
2 cups chocolate chips
1 cup chopped pecans

- Preheat oven to 350°.

- Cream butter, brown sugar and sugar in large bowl and beat in milk, vanilla and eggs. Stir in corn flakes and oats.

- In separate bowl, sift flour, baking soda, 1 teaspoon salt and spices. Gradually add to cookie mixture. (Cookie batter will be very stiff.)

- Stir in coconut, chocolate chips and pecans. Drop teaspoonfuls of dough onto cookie sheet. Bake for 10 to 15 minutes. Yields 5 dozen cookies.

Crunchy Cashew Cookies

1 cup (2 sticks) butter, softened
1 cup sugar
¾ cup packed brown sugar
1 egg
2¼ cups flour
½ teaspoon baking soda
½ teaspoon cream of tartar
2 teaspoons vanilla
1 teaspoon almond extract
1½ cups chopped cashews

- Preheat oven to 350°.

- Combine butter, sugar, brown sugar and egg in bowl and beat
  well. Blend in flour, baking soda and cream of tartar. Add
  vanilla, almond extract and cashews and mix thoroughly.

- Drop teaspoonfuls of dough onto sprayed cookie sheet and
  bake for 10 to 12 minutes or until golden brown. Yields
  3 dozen cookies.

*Los Angeles has the fewest number of freeway miles per
capita of any American city or urbanized area, which accounts
for the congestion on the highways.*

Macadamia Nut Cookies

½ cup shortening
½ cup (1 stick) butter, softened
2½ cups flour, divided
1 cup packed brown sugar
½ cup sugar
2 eggs
1 teaspoon vanilla
½ teaspoon butter flavoring
½ teaspoon baking soda
2 cups white chocolate chips
1 (3 ounce) jar macadamia nuts, chopped

- Preheat oven to 350°.

- Beat shortening and butter in bowl. Add half flour and mix well. Add brown sugar, sugar, eggs, vanilla, butter flavoring and baking soda.

- Beat until mixture combines well. Add remaining flour, mix well and stir in white chocolate chips and nuts.

- Drop teaspoonfuls of dough onto cookie sheet and bake for 8 minutes. Yields 3 dozen cookies.

California is the second most populous state in the Western Hemisphere. The state of Sao Paulo, Brazil is the largest.

White Chocolate-Almond Cookies

¾ cup firmly packed light brown sugar
½ cup sugar
½ cup (1 stick) butter, softened
½ cup shortening
1½ teaspoons vanilla
1 egg
1¾ cups plus 2 tablespoons flour
1 teaspoon baking soda
1 cup white chocolate chips
⅓ cup slivered almonds

- Preheat oven to 350°.

- Combine brown sugar, sugar, butter, shortening, vanilla and egg in large bowl and mix well.

- Stir in flour, baking soda and ½ teaspoon salt and blend well. Stir in white chocolate chips and almonds and mix well. (Batter will be stiff.)

- Drop teaspoonfuls of dough onto cookie sheet and bake for 10 minutes or until they are light golden brown. Store cookies in airtight container. Yields 2½ dozen cookies.

Orange Balls

1 (12 ounce) box vanilla wafers, crushed
½ cup (1 stick) butter, melted
1 (16 ounce) box powdered sugar
1 (6 ounce) can frozen orange juice concentrate, thawed
1 cup finely chopped pecans

- Combine vanilla wafers, butter, powdered sugar and orange juice concentrate in bowl and mix well.

- Roll into balls and roll in chopped pecans. Store in airtight container. Yields 1½ dozen balls.

Apricot-Almond Bars

1 (18 ounce) box yellow cake mix
½ cup (1 stick) butter, melted
¾ cup finely chopped almonds
1 (12 ounce) jar apricot preserves, slightly heated, divided
1 (8 ounce) package cream cheese, softened
¼ cup sugar
2 tablespoons flour
1 egg
1 teaspoon vanilla
⅔ cup flaked coconut

- Combine cake mix and butter in large bowl and mix with spoon until crumbly. Stir in almonds and set aside 1 cup crumb mixture.

- Lightly press crumb mixture into sprayed 9 x 13-inch baking pan. Carefully spread 1 cup preserves over crumb mixture, leaving ¼-inch border.

- Beat cream cheese in bowl until smooth and add remaining preserves, sugar, flour, ⅛ teaspoon salt, egg and vanilla. Carefully spread cream cheese mixture over preserves.

- In separate bowl, combine remaining 1 cup crumb mixture and coconut and mix well. Sprinkle over cream cheese mixture and bake for 35 minutes or until center sets. Cool and store in refrigerator. Yields 20 bars.

In 1902, the first theater to show moving pictures opened in Los Angeles.

Macadamia Bars

Crust:
1 cup (2 sticks) butter, softened
⅔ cup sugar
2 cups flour

- Preheat oven to 350°.

- Cream butter, sugar and flour in bowl. Press into sprayed 9 x 13-inch baking dish and bake for 20 minutes.

Filling:
4 eggs
1 cup flaked coconut
3 cups packed light brown sugar
2 (3.2 ounce) jars macadamia nuts, chopped
¼ cup flour
3 teaspoons vanilla extract
1 teaspoon baking powder

- Lightly beat eggs in medium bowl and add remaining filling ingredients. Pour over hot, baked crust and bake for additional 25 to 30 minutes.

- Cool completely and cut into small squares or you can cut in larger squares and serve with dip of ice cream. Yields 20 bars.

TIP: You could substitute 1½ cups pecans for macadamia nuts. Either way, these bars are moist, chewy and absolutely sinful.

Almond-Coconut Squares

2 cups graham cracker crumbs
3 tablespoons brown sugar
½ cup (1 stick) butter, melted
1 (14 ounce) can sweetened condensed milk
1 (7 ounce) package shredded coconut
1 teaspoon vanilla

- Preheat oven to 325°.

- Combine graham cracker crumbs, brown sugar and butter in
  bowl and mix well. Pat mixture evenly into sprayed
  9 x 13-inch baking pan and bake for 10 minutes. Cool.

- Combine sweetened condensed milk, coconut and vanilla in
  bowl and pour over baked crust. Bake for additional
  25 minutes. Cool.

Topping:

1 (6 ounce) package chocolate chips
1 (6 ounce) package butterscotch chips
¼ cup (½ stick) butter
6 tablespoons crunchy peanut butter
½ cup slivered almonds

- Melt all topping ingredients in double boiler and spread
  mixture over baked ingredients. Cool and cut into squares.
  Yields 20 squares.

*In 1960, Joanne Woodward was the first person to receive a
star on the well known Walk of Fame in Hollywood.*

Buttery Walnut Squares

1 cup (2 sticks) butter, softened
1¾ cups packed brown sugar
1¾ cups flour

- Preheat oven to 350°.

- Combine butter and brown sugar in bowl and beat until smooth and creamy. Add flour and mix well. Pat mixture down evenly in sprayed 9 x 13-inch glass pan and bake for 15 minutes.

Topping:

1 cup packed brown sugar
4 eggs, lightly beaten
2 tablespoons flour
2 cups chopped walnuts
1 cup flaked coconut

- Combine sugar and eggs in medium bowl. Add flour and mix well. Fold in walnuts and coconut and pour over crust.

- Bake for 20 to 25 minutes or until set in center. Cool in pan and cut into squares. Yields 20 squares.

TIP: Serve these delicious squares with a scoop of ice cream for a great dessert.

Lemon-Crumb Squares

⅔ cup (1¼ sticks) butter, softened
½ cup sugar
½ cup packed brown sugar
1½ cups flour
1 teaspoon baking powder
1 cup quick-cooking oats
1 (14 ounce) can sweetened condensed milk
½ cup lemon juice

- Preheat oven to 350°.

- Cream butter, sugar and brown sugar in bowl. Add flour, baking powder, ½ teaspoon salt and oats and beat until mixture is crumbly.

- Spread half mixture in sprayed, floured 9 x 13-inch baking pan and pat down. Set aside remaining mixture.

- In separate bowl, thoroughly mix sweetened condensed milk and lemon juice. Pour over crumbs in baking dish and cover with remaining crumbs.

- Bake for 25 minutes. Cool at room temperature, cut into squares and refrigerate. Yields 20 squares.

Otis Redding wrote his last and greatest hit, "Sitting on the Dock of the Bay" while living in Sausalito on a houseboat.

Caramel-Apple Mousse

¾ cup (1½ sticks) butter
⅔ cup plus ¼ cup sugar, divided
2½ teaspoons lemon juice
½ teaspoon ground cinnamon
2 tablespoons rum
5 - 6 medium apples, peeled, thinly sliced
1 teaspoon vanilla
1 (8 ounce) carton whipped topping, thawed
Peanut brittle, slightly crushed

- Melt butter in large skillet and add ⅔ cup sugar, lemon juice and ¼ cup water. Cook for 10 minutes or until sugar dissolves and syrup is slightly thick and golden; stir often. Remove from heat and add cinnamon, rum and apples.

- Return to heat and cook apples in syrup for 3 to 4 minutes or until they are thoroughly coated and are soft. Remove apples from syrup and cool.

- In separate bowl, add ¼ cup sugar and vanilla to whipped topping and fold apples into whipped topping. Spoon mixture into parfait or crystal sherbet glasses and refrigerate for several hours.

- Sprinkle generously with crushed peanut brittle before serving. Serves 8.

Flan with Caramel Topping

2⅔ cups sugar, divided
8 eggs
1 teaspoon vanilla
½ teaspoon ground cinnamon
1 quart milk, scalded

• Preheat oven to 350°.

• Caramelize 2 cups sugar in saucepan, add 1 tablespoon water and cook for about 1 minute, stirring constantly. Pour caramel into 12 custard cups and tilt each cup to coat sides.

• Beat eggs lightly in bowl and add remaining sugar, vanilla, ¼ teaspoon salt and cinnamon. Stir in milk and pour into custard cups.

• Set cups in pan in about 1 inch hot water and bake for 30 minutes or until a knife near edge comes out clean. Remove flan from molds to serve. Serves 12.

Mango Cream

2 ripe, soft mangos
½ gallon vanilla ice cream, softened
1 (6 ounce) can frozen lemonade concentrate, thawed
1 (8 ounce) carton whipped topping, thawed

• Peel mangoes, cut slices around seed and chop slices. Mix ice cream, lemonade concentrate and whipped topping in large bowl and fold in mango chunks.

• Quickly spoon mixture into parfait glasses, cover with plastic wrap and freeze. Serves 8 to 10.

Mango-Banana Parfaits

1 (15 ounce) can mangos, drained or 1 pound fresh mangos,
   peeled, sliced
2 very ripe bananas, cut in 1-inch slices
¾ cup sour cream
⅓ cup packed brown sugar
1 tablespoon lime juice
1 (8 ounce) carton whipping cream, whipped
2 cups pecans
1 cup sugar
2 teaspoons ground cinnamon

- Cut mangos in chunks and place mangos, bananas, sour cream, brown sugar and lime juice in food processor; puree mixture.

- Pour mixture in bowl and quickly fold in whipped cream. Cover and refrigerate for at least 3 hours or overnight.

- Combine pecans, sugar and cinnamon in large heavy skillet. Cook on medium heat, stirring constantly, until sugar melts.

- Continue cooking until sugar is caramel brown. Pour mixture onto foil-covered baking sheet and spread out to cool. Coarsely chop.

- Do not make parfaits until just before serving. (The crunchy pecans will get soggy if not served immediately).

- To make parfaits in 6 parfait glasses, layer mango-banana mixture and crunchy pecans twice and end with crunchy pecans. Serve immediately. Serves 6.

Index

Cookbooks Published by Cookbook Resources, LLC
Bringing Family and Friends to the Table

Easy Diabetic Recipes

The Best of Cooking with 3 Ingredients

*The Ultimate Cooking
with 4 Ingredients*

Easy Cooking with 5 Ingredients

Gourmet Cooking with 5 Ingredients

*4-Ingredient Recipes
for 30-Minute Meals*

Essential 3-4-5 Ingredient Recipes

The Best 1001 Short, Easy Recipes

1001 Fast Easy Recipes

1001 Community Recipes

Busy Woman's Quick & Easy Recipes

Busy Woman's Slow Cooker Recipes

Easy Slow Cooker Cookbook

Easy One-Dish Meals

Easy Potluck Recipes

Easy Casseroles

Easy Desserts

Sunday Night Suppers

Easy Church Suppers

365 Easy Meals

365 Easy Soups and Stews

365 Easy Vegetarian Recipes

365 Easy Casserole Recipes

365 Easy Chicken Recipes

365 Easy Soup Recipes

365 Easy One-Dish Recipes

365 Easy Pasta Recipes

365 Easy Slow Cooker Recipes

Quick Fixes with Cake Mixes

*Kitchen Keepsakes/More Kitchen
Keepsakes*

Gifts for the Cookie Jar

All New Gifts for the Cookie Jar

Muffins In A Jar

The Big Bake Sale Cookbook

Classic Tex-Mex and Texas Cooking

Classic Southwest Cooking

Miss Sadie's Southern Cooking

Texas Longhorn Cookbook

Cookbook 25 Years

A Little Taste of Texas

A Little Taste of Texas II

Trophy Hunters' Wild Game Cookbook

Recipe Keeper

*Leaving Home Cookbook
and Survival Guide*

Classic Pennsylvania Dutch Cooking

Simple Old-Fashioned Baking

Healthy Cooking with 4 Ingredients

Best-Loved Canadian Recipes

Best-Loved New England Recipes

*Best-Loved Recipes
from the Pacific Northwest*

Best-Loved Southern Recipes

The California Cookbook

The Pennsylvania Cookbook

**cookbook
resources** LLC

www.cookbookresources.com

Your Ultimate Source for Easy Cookbooks

How to Order: **The California Cookbook**

Order online at www.cookbookresources.com

Or Call Toll Free: (866) 229-2665   Or Mail to: Cookbook Resources
            Fax: (972) 317-6404   541 Doubletree Drive
                                                Highland Village, Texas 75077

> **Please note: Shipping/ handling charges may vary according to shipping zone and method.**

Please send ___ copies @ $14.95 (U.S.) each $ _____

Texas residents add sales tax @ $1.23 each $ _____

Plus shipping/handling @ $8.00 (1ˢᵗ copy) $ _____

Plus shipping/handling @ $1.00 per each additional copy $ _____

Check or Credit Card (Canada – credit card only) Total $ _____

Charge to: ☐ MasterCard ☐ VISA   Expiration Date ⌊__⌋ ⌊__⌋ (mm/yy)

Account No. ⌊__⌋ ⌊__⌋ ⌊__⌋ ⌊__⌋

Signature _____

Name (please print) _____

Address _____

City _____ State/Prov. _____ Zip/Postal Code _____

Telephone (Day) _____ (Evening) _____

E-mail Address _____

- - - - - - - - - - - - - - - - - - - -

How to Order: **The California Cookbook**

Order online at www.cookbookresources.com

Or Call Toll Free: (866) 229-2665   Or Mail to: Cookbook Resources
            Fax: (972) 317-6404   541 Doubletree Drive
                                                Highland Village, Texas 75077

> **Please note: Shipping/ handling charges may vary according to shipping zone and method.**

Please send ___ copies @ $14.95 (U.S.) each $ _____

Texas residents add sales tax @ $1.23 each $ _____

Plus shipping/handling @ $8.00 (1ˢᵗ copy) $ _____

Plus shipping/handling @ $1.00 per each additional copy $ _____

Check or Credit Card (Canada – credit card only) Total $ _____

Charge to: ☐ MasterCard ☐ VISA   Expiration Date ⌊__⌋ ⌊__⌋ (mm/yy)

Account No. ⌊__⌋ ⌊__⌋ ⌊__⌋ ⌊__⌋

Signature _____

Name (please print) _____

Address _____

City _____ State/Prov. _____ Zip/Postal Code _____

Telephone (Day) _____ (Evening) _____

E-mail Address _____

Enjoy the latest releases in our
American Regional Series